SKIING SKILLS

SKIING SKILLS

RÜDIGER JAHN

JAN KARLSSON

HERMANN SCHULTES

DOUG PFEIFFER

GROSSET & DUNLAP
A FILMWAYS COMPANY
Publishers • New York

Copyright © 1980 by Nordbok, Gothenburg, Sweden
All rights reserved
Published simultaneously in Canada
Library of Congress catalog card number: 81-47706
ISBN 0-448-11988-9
First Grosset & Dunlap printing 1981
Printed in the United States of America

SKIING SKILLS has been originated and produced by AB Nordbok, Gothenburg, Sweden, in cooperation with the authors and a number of experts and photographers throughout the world.

Editor-in-Chief: Turlough Johnston.

Editor: Kerstin Stålbrand.

Graphical Design: Tommy Berglund.

Skiing Adviser: Ronald Crawford-Currie.

The action drawings have been made by Ulf Söderqvist and are based on photographs specially taken for the purpose by Kjell Langset, Per Klaesson, and Tommy Berglund. The skiing demonstrators were David Alison, New Zealand, Ronald Crawford-Currie, Sweden, Stein Ivar Halsnes, Norway, Bryan Head, Canada, Kjell Langset, Norway, Wilfried Muxel, Austria, Gunilla Öhrn, Sweden, Alasdair Ross, Scotland, and Daniel Sweet, United States. The other drawings were made by Syed Mumtaz Ahmad, Hans Linder, and Lennart Molin.

Photographs: Ulf Blomberg, pages 102–103; Kjell Langset, pages 70–71, 90, 136; Mats Lindgren, pages 2–3, 6, 9, 17, 24–25, 27, 53, 66, 67, 75, 87, 90, 98, 104, 106–107, 137, 144, 154–155, 157; Roland Thorbjörnsson, page 60.

Lithographics: Nils Hermansson.

THE AUTHORS

Rüdiger Jahn has written the four chapters on how to ski: *The Basics, The Able Skier, The Accomplished Skier,* and *Competitive Alpine Skiing.* He is a certified ski instructor in the United States (Professional Ski Instructors Association) and in Austria (Staatlich geprüfter Skilehrer), a member of the United States Coaches Association, and director of the racing camp at Hunter Mountain, New York.

Jan Karlsson has written *Be Prepared.* He is a professor at the Department of Clinical Physiology at the Karolinska Hospital, Stockholm, where he is director of the Laboratory of Human Performance.

Hermann Schultes, who has written *Equipment,* is a well-known consultant in ski technology. He has written several publications in the field and is chairman of the terminology working groups in ASTM and ISO.

Doug Pfeiffer has written *The Ski Resort.* He is an American skier and journalist. He has contributed articles to ski magazines all over the world, his special interest being travel and the ski resort.

Material for the illustrations and captions on pages 44–45 has been provided by Sven Coomer, an internationally recognized authority on the ski boot. The Winchester Press has kindly allowed us to use their book *Freestyle Skiing* as reference for pages 108–109.

CONTENTS

preface

Ski fever is spreading all over the world, much to our joy. Every year, new slopes are opened to cope with the ever-increasing flow of ski-hungry people. They are the ones who, as the season approaches, get that faraway look in their eyes at the mention of snow, begin to take the stairs instead of the elevator, and start jogging every day in preparation for the first run of the season.

People go downhill skiing for many reasons. Some people ski for the challenge involved in, say, mastering a mogul field or skiing in deep powder on untracked slopes; others go for the speed and the excitement; still others go for the solitude of the mountain peaks and for that feeling of being at one with nature; and still others go for the fun of it all, especially the *après-ski*. All regard their sport as something particularly wonderful.

We who have written this book have all been skiing since childhood; yet we still feel the pulses quicken when the first snow falls and still experience the total joy of skiing as we take the slopes of a favorite resort. The best wish we can make is that the readers of this book will feel the same.

The Authors

1

BE
PREPARED

When you start alpine ski-ing, you discover that you are using muscles that you never thought you had! Indicated here are some of the major muscles used, and further on in this chapter, we will show you how to train your "skiing" muscles.

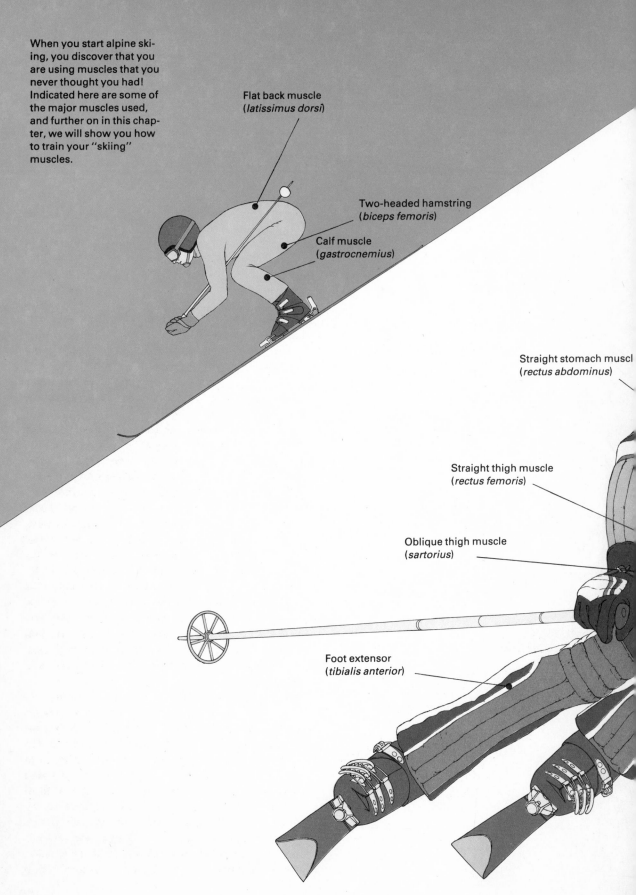

Flat back muscle
(*latissimus dorsi*)

Two-headed hamstring
(*biceps femoris*)

Calf muscle
(*gastrocnemius*)

Straight stomach muscl
(*rectus abdominus*)

Straight thigh muscle
(*rectus femoris*)

Oblique thigh muscle
(*sartorius*)

Foot extensor
(*tibialis anterior*)

Outer thigh muscle
(*vastus lateralis*)

Downhill skiing, or, to give it its more correct name, alpine skiing, is a fast and exciting sport that gives those who partake in it plenty of opportunity for exercise and recreation. The title of this chapter is self-explanatory; to enjoy your skiing thoroughly and in safety, you must go out on the slopes in good condition. Otherwise, you will rapidly become too tired to enjoy it, or, if bad luck strikes, you will pull a muscle and spend the rest of your skiing trip *hors de combat*.

Throughout the industrial world, leisure time has increased, and there is an increasing desire to fill it with some meaningful occupation. Taking part in various forms of sporting activity is one way of adding stimulus to your leisure time, but the circumstances in which you can do this vary widely. Your own individual circumstances—interest, aptitude, etc.—are as important as the external circumstances of climate, geographical environment, etc. Summer and winter sports activities are becoming available to more and more people, giving the possibility of active recreation throughout the year. Skiing is an increasingly popular sport that has become the major winter sport for many people in both hemispheres.

What makes one decide to choose a particular form of exercise? We have already mentioned the personal and external circumstances, but at least as important as these is the marketing of the sport in question. It is not difficult to find the connection between the number of participants of a sport and the coverage given to that sport by newspapers, TV, radio, and advertising. For better or for worse, the "prestige sports" set the pattern and provide the stimulus for older keep-fit sportsmen and for the young, from whose ranks the champions of the future are recruited. For instance, interest in alpine skiing has grown enormously during the 1960s and 1970s, and the part played in this growth by Karl Schranz, Jean-Claude Killy, Franz Klammer, Gustavo Thöni, Phil Mahre, Ingemar Stenmark, and others is obvious.

Many of us do not exercise properly in our daily work, and especially we do not give those muscles we use in skiing enough exercise. The skeletal musculature is the system of muscles and skeleton forming the moving apparatus that enables us to move our bodies. It is the largest volume of tissue in the body. The muscle cells, or fibers, that form the muscles are microscopically small units containing systems that can transform chemically bound energy (found, for instance, in sugar and fat) into mechanical work. In a way, muscle fibers function like a combustion engine. Fuel in a combustion

the capacity to convert their slow fibers into quick in training, will be able to succeed at cross-country skiing or running. Sports research has confirmed the importance both of inherited tendencies and of so-called fiber conversion to success at top-level sport.

Percentage of slow fibers in the thigh muscles

0   20   40   60   80   100

- cross-country skiing
- walking
- alpine skiing
- ice hockey

The Body's Engines

When your muscles work, the chemical energy that is bound up in the muscles' fuels (sugar and fat) is transformed into mechanical energy. This breakdown of the sugar and the fat in your muscles normally takes place with the assistance of the oxygen that is inside each muscle cell. This process of breakdown with the help of oxygen is known as the aerobic process. We can call this the body's combustion engine. The muscle cells receive their oxygen via the body's circulatory apparatus, in which the heart functions as a pump. This method of transporting oxygen to the muscles has certain advantages from the biological point of view, but there are also disadvantages. Bees and other insects have no lungs or circulatory apparatus; their working muscles are in direct contact with the outside air, which means that they can be rapidly supplied with oxygen. With a human being it is

engine is consumed under explosive conditions, and the chemical energy released sets a piston in motion; a transformation into mechanical work takes place.

There are two main types of muscle fiber: fast and slow. As the name implies, fast fibers can contract quicker than slow. The proportions of slow muscle fibers in the thigh muscles of some different sportsmen is shown above. The properties of the slow fiber, for instance endurance, mean that the advanced cross-country skier has a high percentage of this type of fiber in his muscles. About eighty percent of a cross-country skier's muscles are of slow fibers. Jumpers and throwers represent the opposite extreme, with about sixty percent fast and forty percent slow fibers. The average person has about fifty percent of each type and, strangely enough, the top-class alpine skier has the same, which may be interpreted as meaning that alpine skiing makes no special demands on the composition of the muscle fibers. This would be wrong, however; it is closer to the truth to say that top-class alpine skiing makes great demands on endurance, agility, and strength, which means that both the slow and the fast fibers are used intensively. On the other hand, the cross-country man depends almost exclusively on his slow muscle fibers, while throwers and jumpers are largely dependent on their fast fibers. Broadly speaking, only people who have a high proportion of slow muscle fibers from the outset, or who have

The effect produced by the muscle's combustion engine is determined by the individual's capacity to inhale oxygen and transport it to the muscles. The diagram here compares the capacities of well-trained athletes in different sports and that of a healthy but unfit person. The intake of oxygen is measured in ml/kg/min, that is, milliliters per kilogram of weight and per minute.

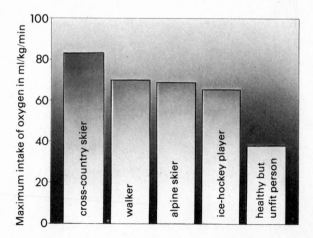

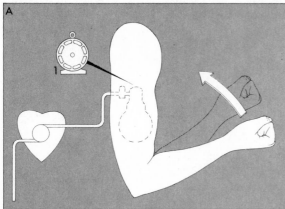

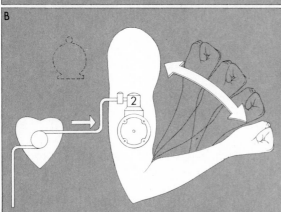

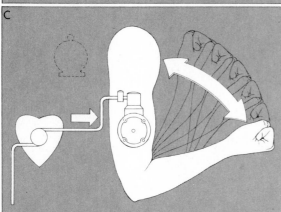

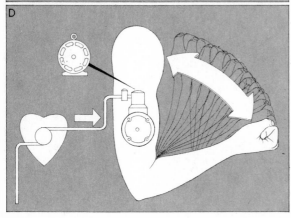

A Starting a movement "cold" means that the combustion engine, in which the heart acts as a circulation pump, cannot get under way immediately, so the lactic-acid engine (*1*) must provide the necessary effect.

B As the muscles warm up, the combustion engine (*2*) takes over, and the lactic-acid engine shuts down.

C As the activity increases and makes greater demands on the muscles, the combustion engine can still supply enough oxygen to the muscles to keep everything flowing smoothly.

D When a sudden and intensive effort is necessary, the combustion engine cannot supply the demand, so the lactic-acid engine is automatically coupled in.

different. When he engages in hard work, the oxygen necessary is transported to the muscles along the circulatory apparatus, and this is not capable of carrying sufficient oxygen to hard-working muscles. To make up for this deficiency of oxygen, the muscles are equipped with an "auxiliary engine," which works without oxygen. This function is known as the anaerobic process, and it produces lactic acid in the muscles. Lactid acid affects a number of factors and processes, both locally, in the working muscle, and more centrally, for instance in the brain, and this causes a feeling of physical fatigue.

The amount of energy that a human being can produce depends on how powerful the two engines are. The effect produced by the combustion engine (the aerobic processes) is determined by the amount of oxygen the individual can inhale and transport to the muscles, and this is determined by the capacity of the circulatory apparatus, the center of which is the pump, or heart. The size of the heart varies from individual to individual. Similarly, the structure of the circulatory system varies from individual to individual, and this is the biological reason why one person's capacity for strenuous activity is greater than another's. In order not to dishearten the unfit skier who wants to improve his condition, it is important to emphasize that training *does* improve the effectiveness of the pump and the regulation of the pumping system. However, only in exceptional cases will there be more than a twenty percent improvement; it is important to possess an inborn aptitude, in other words, to "choose the right parents."

There are several ways of showing how effective the heart is. One is to measure the maximum amount of oxygen that a person can inhale and transport to the working muscles per unit of time; this value is given in liters per minute or in milliliters per kilo per minute. In the latter case the individual's body weight is also taken into account;

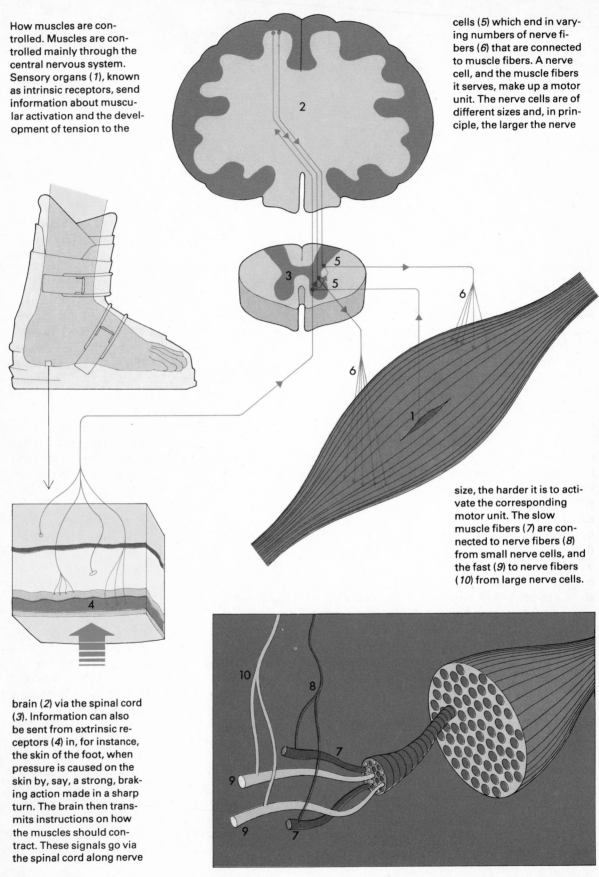

How muscles are controlled. Muscles are controlled mainly through the central nervous system. Sensory organs (*1*), known as intrinsic receptors, send information about muscular activation and the development of tension to the cells (*5*) which end in varying numbers of nerve fibers (*6*) that are connected to muscle fibers. A nerve cell, and the muscle fibers it serves, make up a motor unit. The nerve cells are of different sizes and, in principle, the larger the nerve size, the harder it is to activate the corresponding motor unit. The slow muscle fibers (*7*) are connected to nerve fibers (*8*) from small nerve cells, and the fast (*9*) to nerve fibers (*10*) from large nerve cells.

brain (*2*) via the spinal cord (*3*). Information can also be sent from extrinsic receptors (*4*) in, for instance, the skin of the foot, when pressure is caused on the skin by, say, a strong, braking action made in a sharp turn. The brain then transmits instructions on how the muscles should contract. These signals go via the spinal cord along nerve

this is of interest to the marathon runner, for instance, but is of less importance to swimmers, canoeists, and others who do not have to "carry" their bodies but float in or on water.

The effect produced by the "auxiliary engine" (the anaerobic processes) depends on how much lactic acid the individual produces. This in turn is determined by how much muscle he has and on how much lactic acid the muscles will tolerate. The short-distance runner is often more athletically built than the marathon runner, which is partly explained by the fact that the former is more dependent on the lactic-acid, or auxiliary, engine. The effects of lactic acid on the body can be influenced and controlled in several ways. For instance, the muscles can be "taught" to tolerate a large dose of lactic acid. Also, the body can be trained to speed up the removal of the lactic acid to other parts of the body, such as the liver, the heart, and inactive muscles, where its fatiguing effect on the body in general is reduced. Lactic-acid training programs are devoted to increasing the total capacity of the organism in these respects.

Research has shown that sports involving a brief, intensive effort make greater demands on the lactic-acid engine than sports demanding a more long-term effort and in which endurance is an important factor; in the long-term-effort type of sports, the combustion engine is put to more use than the lactic-acid engine. For the short, intensive effort, the lactic-acid engine is best, as it can be started and accelerated faster than the combustion engine, which is dependent on the whole circulatory apparatus getting into operation, something that may take up to three minutes; then you get your "second wind." (For someone who is properly warmed up, this may take as little as thirty to sixty seconds.) As previously mentioned, the lactic acid formed by the lactic-acid engine causes a sensation of tiredness, and this is why the body tries to achieve as much as possible of its energy conversion with its combustion engine.

Alpine skiing involves a more or less continuous intensive effort for all skiers, whether beginners or experts. So however skilled the skier, both the combustion and the lactic-acid engines are important, and a first-class skier will have both a highly developed capacity for inhaling and transporting oxygen to the muscles, and a highly effective lactic-acid engine. In this respect, he is comparable to the top-class athlete in a sport that demands maximum energy transformation for a period of up to a few minutes—running 400 or 800 m, swimming 100 or 200 m, and so forth.

Technique

But is alpine skiing not primarily a question of technique? This question must occur above all to the beginner who has been working at perfecting his "ski-school turns" and at last feels that "Now I've got it!". The answer is, of course, yes; skiing is definitely a matter of technique, no matter at what level it is performed. However, the technique itself and the demands made on it vary according to the degree of skill that is desired. There is a difference between the ways in which the leisure skier and the advanced skier ski, but naturally, both try to exploit their technical prowess to the full. There is no doubt that part of the fascination of alpine skiing is the challenge that every skier feels to excel himself. The various disciplines—slalom, giant slalom, downhill racing, and freestyle—make great demands on individual technique, but it should be emphasized that the ways in which top-level skiers fulfil the demands made on their technical ability vary from person to person, according to individual circumstances, basic schooling, etc. Many people, including some sports writers, tend to judge a skier's technique on purely aesthetic grounds, and this can lead to the wrong conclusions being drawn about technique.

Muscular strength is a cornerstone of technique, but how it is used and deployed is also important. Another aspect of technique is a "feel" for snow and slope conditions; this is partly a matter of experience and partly a matter of the inbuilt ability to let the muscles react properly in terms of time, speed, and tension (these three usually fall under the heading "timing," which is largely dependent on inherited qualities in the receptors in the muscles and tendons; these receptors send information to the brain about tension development in the muscles and joints). The problem is, of course, that skiing is seasonal, so at the start of each season, you have to acquire anew that "feel," and this takes time and practice on the slopes.

Basically, muscular strength is determined by two things: the thickness of the muscle (its cross-section) and the type of muscle fiber that predominates. In addition, the whole muscle—or as much of it as possible—must be able to contract. The muscle contracts in response to electrical signals which reach it via the nervous system (see p. 14). Muscular activity—rest, contraction, rest, and so on—is called *motoricity*. Each motor nerve is connected to a number of muscle fibers of the same type, making a motor unit. In this way, the entire muscle is innervated and is equipped with motor units with various characteristics. The slow motor

15

units are the easiest to activate and take part in almost all muscular movement. The quick motor units come into use when more muscle power is required, or if the movement is particularly rapid. In the case of extremely fast muscle movements, only the quick motor units are used. The various motor units are thus used differently, according to their different characteristics and according to the occasion.

As indicated already, many of the qualities that determine speed, strength, etc. are hereditary, but this does not mean that training is pointless, even at the level of the person who skis for fun. An important part of training lies in teaching the body its own limitations and how to act in accordance with them. In addition, the results that training has on strength and fitness are far from incidental to a skier's natural aptitude.

Technique, however, does not mean only strength and muscle-fiber recruitment. Other factors are important, too. For instance, you must know when, where, and how to exert that strength, and it is the higher nerve centers that are involved here. The brain processes information it receives on, for example, speed and steepness of slope and converts it into motor activity. Moreover, the muscle itself is sensitive to the power it develops. For instance, if you come to a hollow you have not noticed, your body will still function (or, at least, try to function!) so that you will not lose your skiing rhythm or even fall. All the information about the hollow is fed into the brain and compared with the information, based on skill and experience, that is stored there already. The result is a decision of which you are not always conscious, as the decision is made very quickly and in the parts of the brain which give you your "geographical" awareness, that is, how you perceive the relative positions of the different parts of your body. These very important functions of the body are generally summarized under the term "physical anticipation." Such anticipation is one of the most important characteristics of the good skier, as it is decisive in correcting directional errors, and the necessary corrections must take place simultaneously and at or near maximum power. Therefore, the fast muscle fibers play a very important role in such situations.

The individual's capacity for learning to ski varies in the same way as his capacity for, say, ball games like tennis, football, and golf, in which a good ball-sense is important. Basically, the same talents that determine how good our ball-sense is also determine how well we can ski. The nerve centers responsible for anticipation are better developed in some people, which is why many top-class skiers have an almost acrobatic talent for tight-rope walking, trick cycling, etc.

The electric signals that decide when the muscle is to contract can be recorded in various ways. Electromyography, EMG for short, is the general term used to cover this technique. A skier's electromyogram can be recorded on a portable tape recorder while he is actually skiing. If we compare

EMG comparisons show that an advanced skier rests his "skiing" muscles more often than a leisure skier does when negotiating turns (1). The muscles shown are the outer thigh muscle, *vastus lateralis* (2), the muscle of the back of the arm, *triceps surae* (3), the foot extensor, *tibialis anterior* (4), and the straight stomach muscle, *rectus abdominus* (5).

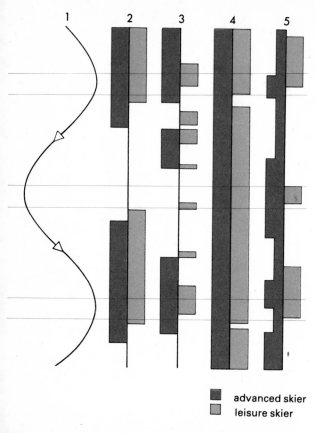

advanced skier
leisure skier

an advanced skier's EMG with that of a leisure skier, we find that the former's EMG shows short periods with and without electrical activity, that is, periods when the muscle is working and resting, respectively. The working periods coincide with the skier's turns. The leisure skier shows quite a different EMG pattern that is much more irregular, with longer contraction times in certain muscles, that is, these muscles are not allowed to rest. Thanks to the short, frequent resting periods, known as micropauses, the advanced skier's muscle can function at almost full capacity for long periods. It is during these micropauses that the muscle absorbs new, oxygen-rich blood and metabolic waste products such as carbon dioxide are removed. When the muscle contracts, the blood cannot circulate so well or even stops circulating, due to the fact that the blood vessels become powerfully compressed. The inexperienced leisure skier's back and leg muscles are convulsively cramped all the time when he is skiing, which is one of the reasons why the beginner looks undynamic and stiff. Other reasons are fear and lack of self-confidence.

Summing up, we can now say that, from the physiological point of view, the following is required of the skier:

1 Transformation of energy; this gives the muscle its strength and is achieved by the combustion engine (aerobic energy transformation) and by the lactic-acid engine (anaerobic energy transformation).

2 Strength and agility; these depend on the power developed by the muscle and on the speed at which it produces power.

3 Movement alertness and coordination; these give the advanced skier's movements a dance-like appearance.

Training

The combustion engine is dependent on the transport of oxygen to the muscles, and here, the condition of the individual is decisive. It is very important to underline that the leisure skier, who is interested in skiing three or four hours a day for five days or so of his week's skiing holiday, needs to train in such a way that his combustion engine, and not his lactic-acid engine, is brought into trim.

Whether you are a beginner or an advanced leisure skier, you should base your fitness on year-round training. Get into condition by jogging, cross-country skiing, swimming, cycling, etc. A

Each of these exercises is designed to strengthen a "skiing" muscle, as indicated. Try to do each ten times, but don't overdo it in the beginning.

A Lie on back with knees bent and both arms stretched to the right. Sit up, pivoting upper body to the right. Lie down slowly. Repeat to the left.

B Lie on back, with legs bent and hands behind head. Raise upper body to knees, keeping bent arms *straight out* from body. Lie down slowly.

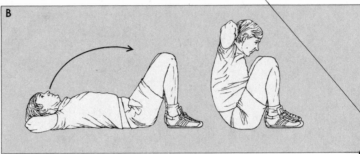

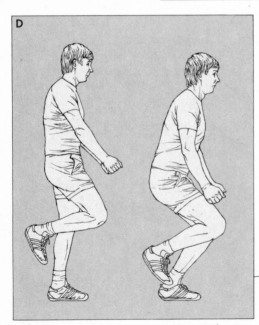

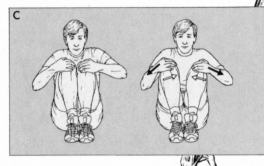

C Sit with knees drawn up in front of you with hands on the insides of knees. Press knees together while holding them apart with hands.

D Stand on left leg. Bend left knee slowly. Stay down as long as you can. Repeat with right leg.
E Sit on floor with left leg bent and right leg straight. Get someone to hold your stretched right foot at the toe. Straighten foot against this pressure. Repeat with left leg.

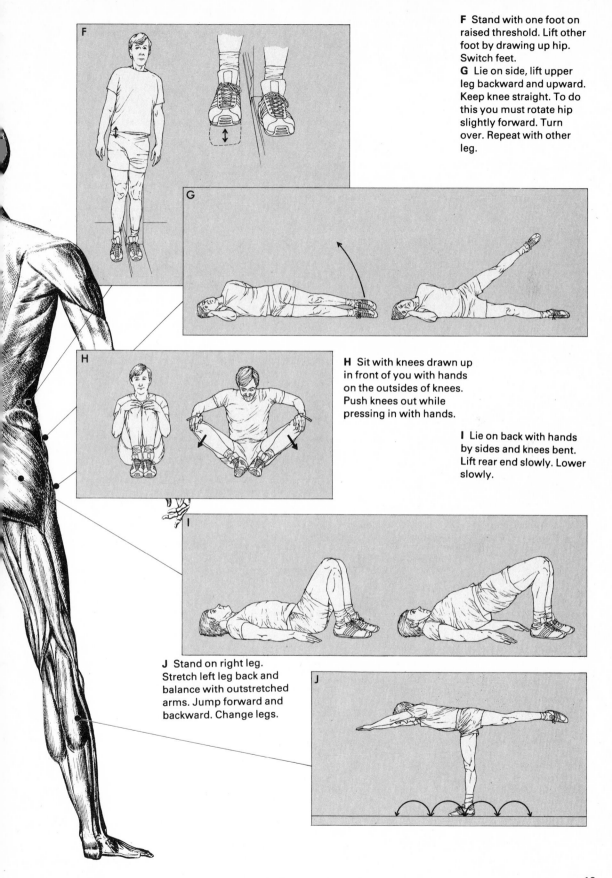

F Stand with one foot on raised threshold. Lift other foot by drawing up hip. Switch feet.

G Lie on side, lift upper leg backward and upward. Keep knee straight. To do this you must rotate hip slightly forward. Turn over. Repeat with other leg.

H Sit with knees drawn up in front of you with hands on the outsides of knees. Push knees out while pressing in with hands.

I Lie on back with hands by sides and knees bent. Lift rear end slowly. Lower slowly.

J Stand on right leg. Stretch left leg back and balance with outstretched arms. Jump forward and backward. Change legs.

The following exercises not only strengthen muscles, they also stretch them and help you to improve your balance.

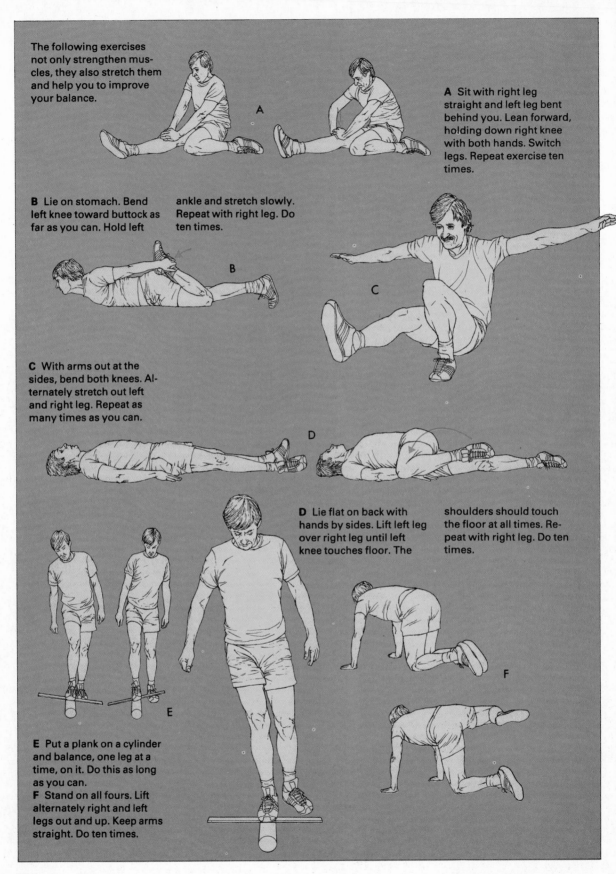

A Sit with right leg straight and left leg bent behind you. Lean forward, holding down right knee with both hands. Switch legs. Repeat exercise ten times.

B Lie on stomach. Bend left knee toward buttock as far as you can. Hold left ankle and stretch slowly. Repeat with right leg. Do ten times.

C With arms out at the sides, bend both knees. Alternately stretch out left and right leg. Repeat as many times as you can.

D Lie flat on back with hands by sides. Lift left leg over right leg until left knee touches floor. The shoulders should touch the floor at all times. Repeat with right leg. Do ten times.

E Put a plank on a cylinder and balance, one leg at a time, on it. Do this as long as you can.
F Stand on all fours. Lift alternately right and left legs out and up. Keep arms straight. Do ten times.

Jogging is an excellent way of improving your movement alertness—and it's fun to do, too! No special equipment is really necessary, you can go jogging almost anywhere, and young and old alike can do it.

21

Outdoor training should consist of exercises that imitate the skier's actions on snow.

(3) "Crouch hopping" up or down a slope strengthens the "skiing" muscles and improves balance.

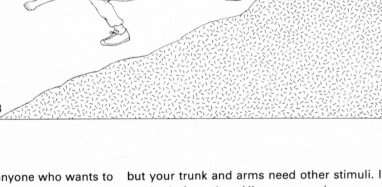

(1) "Traversing" down a hill and (2) "slaloming" between trees improve balance and timing.

general recommendation for anyone who wants to become reasonably fit is to train two to three half-hours a week. The greater your ambition, the more time you spend training. As mentioned above, lactic-acid training is not so important for the leisure skier, but you will improve your lactic-acid engine somewhat if you go in for strength and agility training, although this training will mainly improve the combustion engine. Further improvements can be made by a gradual increase in the intensity of your training in the weeks before the skiing season begins.

Strength and agility training is the most important kind of training for the leisure skier, who is normally a sedentary worker. Sedentary work has more negative effects on strength and agility than on fitness. If you concentrate on improving your fitness by running, your legs will become stronger, but your trunk and arms need other stimuli. In the weeks before the skiing season (or your skiing holiday) begins, you should set aside a few hours every week for gymnastics that will increase your strength and agility.

Exercises to increase movement alertness and fitness are important not only to your skiing, but also to your safety, because in this way you reduce the dangers of injuring yourself in a fall. This applies above all to older people who are learning to ski. Physical activity is in itself an exercise in movement alertness. Jogging, for instance, is excellent. Advanced gymnastics are good for those who want to go even further. Judo wrestlers' falling techniques are sometimes recommended as an aid to those skiers who want to improve their movement alertness.

Opportunities for indoor training under expert

supervison are becoming more generally available through sporting organizations, schools, etc. If there is no keep-fit group near you, or if you prefer to train at home, the exercises given here will help to improve your strength and movement alertness.

Remember to take each movement slowly. Fast snatching or flinging movements may damage tendons or muscles, and will cause unnecessary stiffness afterward. Do the exercises until you feel a definite tiredness in the muscles you have activated, but don't overdo it. Take a few minutes' active rest after each exercise. Try some mild jogging or jazz-ballet movements; this uses large groups of muscles and the feeling of tiredness will vanish after a few minutes, so that you can start the next exercise. After a time you can extend this basic program by improvising new movements or adding new exercises.

Diet

What to eat when skiing is a matter of some importance to the skier. As we have said, skiing is an activity that causes high energy transformation, which in itself is positive for those of us who are trying to keep our weight down. But the high level of physical activity involved can lead to a problem of fuel deficiency for the skier when he runs out of the necessary muscle fuel; this usually happens because he has failed to top up on his fuel supply by not eating the proper food.

Although fat and sugar are both fuels, there is a difference between them. To put it simply, fat is low octane fuel, while sugar is high octane. The more vigorous the muscular activity, the greater the amount of fuel needed, and only sugar is used in vigorous activity. Sugar is stored in the muscles and the liver, while a very small proportion is stored in the blood. The total amount of sugar stored is relatively small and can be used up in a few hours of hard, continuous exercise, such as long-distance running or cross-country skiing. Although the alpine skier is not continuously active in the same way, there is still a danger that he can exhaust the sugar in his energy tank, especially the sugar stored in the muscles. One of the first results of early biochemical research in this field confirmed the definite connection between physical tiredness and muscle-sugar deficiency, with the consequence of a considerable drop in the capacity for hard work.

Intense participation in ski-school training can, in principle, lead to muscle-sugar deficiency. This leads to a deterioration in the activity of the muscles, with a consequent diminishing of movement alertness and the ensuing risk of injury. So muscle-sugar deficiency must be avoided, and the way to do this is to plan your intake of food correctly. Basically, you should increase the proportion of carbohydrates in your food by eating more fruit and foods based on flour (spaghetti, pancakes etc.). Don't forget that it takes time for muscles to take up and store sugar, normally twenty-four to thirty-six hours if the supply is completely exhausted. Another thing to remember is that this process must not be disturbed—by alcohol, for instance. The small amount of alcohol in one beer is enough to produce a measurable effect on the process. This means that vigorous skiing should not be combined with an over-generous intake of alcohol. This presents a problem for the leisure skier, who often combines his skiing with his holiday (and the après-ski socializing that a skiing holiday entails). If you want to drink, drink with moderation in the evening (this said at the expense of sounding a kill-joy!) and not at all during the day's skiing, if you want to get the most out of your skiing.

Another reason for avoiding alcohol in association with skiing is its negative effect on the nervous system and on movement alertness. Medicinally, alcohol has a narcotic effect that slows down the individual's reaction time and impairs his precision of movement. Naturally, this increases the risk of injury, and if you remember that alcohol also impairs the judgment, then that risk becomes even more obvious.

Another factor that has an adverse effect on athletic ability is smoking, as it affects the capacity of the blood to absorb and transport oxygen to the active groups of muscles. The deterioration is generally considered to be ten percent, but there are great individual differences. An impaired oxygen supply means that the combustion engine cannot function properly, and so stamina deteriorates. In addition, the need for the auxiliary engine increases; this means that lactic acid is produced, and this accumulates in the active muscles and leads to impaired muscle function and hence reduced movement alertness. If you can, avoid smoking during your skiing holiday; if this is too much to ask, then abstain from smoking for one to two hours before you go skiing. This will normalize the blood's capacity to transport oxygen (it takes one to two hours to get rid of the carbon monoxide that is always present in a smoker's blood, inhibiting the red blood corpuscles from transporting oxygen).

Clothing

Muscles work better when they are warm, so see to it that you are properly clothed, and keep warm during the day's skiing. The leisure skier does not need to warm up especially, because as long as he is properly dressed, the activity of organizing his equipment and getting into and out of the ski lift is sufficient to warm up the muscles. However, if the temperature is low and if a wind is blowing, the cold can cause problems. Your clothing should, therefore, protect you from getting chilled, for instance when you are sitting in the lift. On the other hand, too much clothing can also be a problem. If you go in for hard skiing, a lot of heat builds up in

(*LEFT*) Diagram showing how your working capacity diminishes (in comparison to the normal) when you lose body fluid through sweating. Compensate for this fluid loss by drinking lots of fluid during your day's skiing.
(*RIGHT*) The three-layer principle of clothing. Layer 1 transports sweat away from the skin, layer 2 absorbs it, and layer 3 insulates and protects.

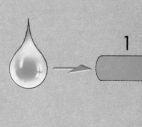

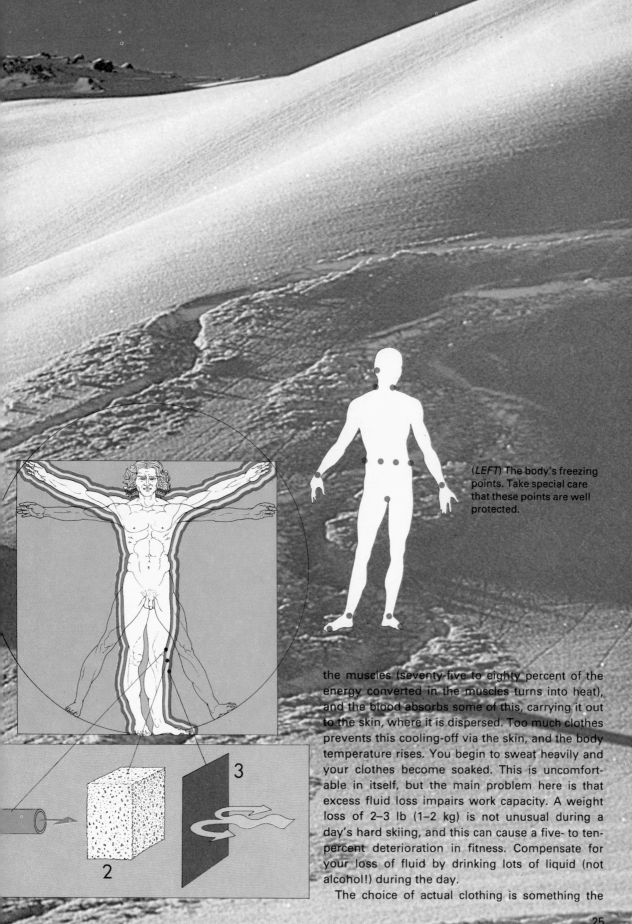

(*LEFT*) The body's freezing points. Take special care that these points are well protected.

the muscles (seventy-five to eighty percent of the energy converted in the muscles turns into heat), and the blood absorbs some of this, carrying it out to the skin, where it is dispersed. Too much clothes prevents this cooling-off via the skin, and the body temperature rises. You begin to sweat heavily and your clothes become soaked. This is uncomfortable in itself, but the main problem here is that excess fluid loss impairs work capacity. A weight loss of 2–3 lb (1–2 kg) is not unusual during a day's hard skiing, and this can cause a five- to ten-percent deterioration in fitness. Compensate for your loss of fluid by drinking lots of liquid (not alcohol!) during the day.

The choice of actual clothing is something the

skier must decide for himself. He will find from experience that certain combinations of clothing give him just the freedom and protection from the cold that he wants. If you are a beginner, follow the advice of your skiing instructor. Here, however, are some general tips. The most sensitive parts of the body should be well protected, but some ventilation next to the skin must be provided for. Base your choice of clothing on the three-layer principle. The garments closest to your body—not least those on your feet—should be of a type which carries sweat outward, thus keeping your skin dry. Wool (if you can stand wearing it next to your skin) is a good material for those garments, and some of the new synthetic materials are even better. Layer number two should absorb humidity, and the topmost layer should insulate and protect. Temperature and wind force will then have to decide how much in the way of pullovers, anoraks, and jackets the top layer should consist of. Remember that damp clothes considerably increase the risk of frostbite.

"Keep your feet warm!" is a very sound piece of advice, because if your feet get cold, they will lose their sense of feeling, and this will affect your sense of balance. Some kind of head gear is advisable, because it is through the head that the percentually greatest part of the body's heat loss goes. That is why a hat on your head will help to keep your feet warm!

So now you know how to get fit enough to enjoy your skiing, what you should eat when you are skiing, and how to keep warm when you are on the slopes. All that now remains is what it's all about—SKIING!

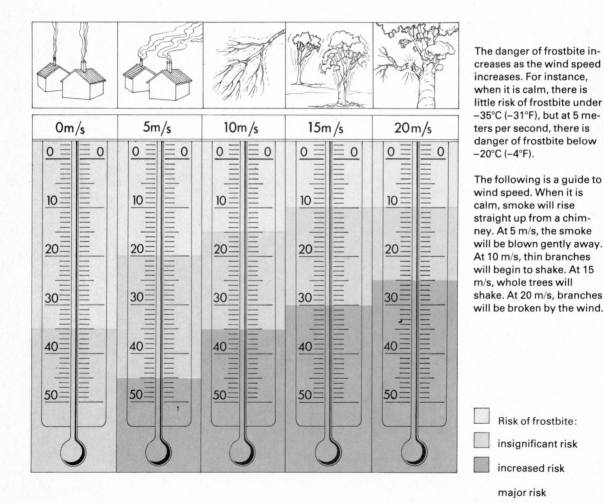

The danger of frostbite increases as the wind speed increases. For instance, when it is calm, there is little risk of frostbite under −35°C (−31°F), but at 5 meters per second, there is danger of frostbite below −20°C (−4°F).

The following is a guide to wind speed. When it is calm, smoke will rise straight up from a chimney. At 5 m/s, the smoke will be blown gently away. At 10 m/s, thin branches will begin to shake. At 15 m/s, whole trees will shake. At 20 m/s, branches will be broken by the wind.

Risk of frostbite:

insignificant risk

increased risk

major risk

2

EQUIPMENT

Alpine skiing requires more sophisticated equipment than most other popular sports. Today's expert skier would not at all be satisfied with the performance of the equipment used just one decade ago. Since then, skiers have stepped up their demands on equipment: they want better performance, more comfort, and increased standards of safety. Happily, the industry has developed apace, and the simple materials of the "pioneer age" have been substituted by masterpieces of modern technology. The continuing exertions by manufacturers to produce designs that give improved performance not only benefit racers and other top-class skiers, but also contribute consider-

ably to the quality of the equipment available to the recreational skier. The high degree of sophistication of modern ski equipment is manifest in the publicity given to the "equipment battles" prior to World Cup events or Olympic Games.

This competition between the leading equipment manufacturers and the oversupply of good equipment have produced positive as well as negative results. The technical standard of the ski equipment now available is very high, and there is hardly any really bad equipment on the market. On the other hand, the customer is faced with the task of selecting the best from this oversupply of products. Another of the negative aspects of today's

A simplified explanation of the principle of alpine skiing. An alpine ski must glide with very little resistance in the longitudinal direction, that is, the frictional force F_G must be small. The frictional (steering) forces F_S, acting on the steel edges in the lateral direction, must be great and variable through edge-setting of the skis. These forces can be said to consist of two components, F_{S1} and F_{S2}, representing the sum of the frictional forces acting on the steel

F_{s1}

F_{s2}

situation is the trend toward mass production and its related distribution methods. The need to sell their overproduction can induce manufacturers to conduct misleading advertising campaigns, and such marketing pressures cause confusion, making it difficult for the serious buyer to distinguish between gimmickry and true quality features. A skier, whether beginner or accomplished, who is looking for optimal equipment, is therefore well advised to use the services of a shop that is specialized in skiing equipment. The sales personnel of such a shop will be familiar with the performance characteristics of their merchandise. They will have tried out the different equipment and will be up-to-date

edge behind and in front of the ski's pivoting point, X, respectively. The skier controls the turning moment caused by these forces by shifting his center of mass in the longitudinal direction.

F_G

on modern trends and innovations. However, the careful buyer will only profit from his discussions with the sales people if he is able to understand the basics of ski equipment technology. It is the purpose of this chapter to provide such basics, so that the skier can select equipment that best suits his requirements.

The Technical Definition of Alpine Skiing

In order to understand fully the importance of equipment to modern alpine skiing, it is necessary to be familiar with a few of the basic mechanics of the sport. Alpine skiing is defined as a combined motion in longitudinal and lateral directions. The balance of the lateral motion (the skidding phase) is used to control direction and speed.

The Interrelationship between Equipment and Performance

In high-performance skiing, especially in racing, the skier must sense changes in the terrain and in snow conditions within fractions of a second, in order to react properly and to direct the skis in the desired direction at the desired speed. The essential steering actions are shift of weight in the longitudinal direction, change of edge-set angle, and weighting or unweighting maneuvers. All these measures are used to control the system of forces acting on the bottom edge (bottom surface). The response to the steering action applied must be precise, so that the line carved down the hill will be perfect. An unintended reaction from the ski will cause immediate trouble. Modern ski equipment is designed with the objective that steering impulses given by the skier will be more directly transferred to the ski, thus increasing the precision, ease, and predictability of the skiing maneuvers.

The Functional Unit: Ski–Boot–Binding

Steering actions will result in precise skiing maneuvers only if all parts of the equipment work together as a functional unit. The designers of skis, boots, and bindings cooperate closely to tune the performance characteristics of their products according to the latest trends in skiing techniques. When properly selected, the products of leading manufacturers will work together as one system. It is vital that all three parts of the system meet the same level of quality and performance. The best high-performance ski does not work well if combined with a cheap, low-performance boot. The same is true for a high-quality heel-and-toe-unit release binding, whose important safety features will not work if a boot with a worn sole is used.

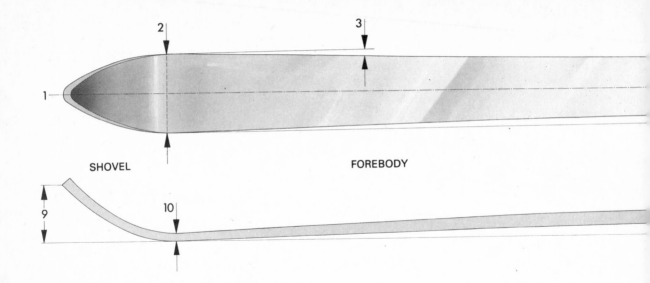

SHOVEL   FOREBODY

The Alpine Ski

That time is now long gone when it was the primary task of a designer to build a solid ski that would survive the tremendous punishment of alpine skiing. Excellent durability, resulting in a long life span, is a matter of course for the modern alpine ski. The challenge now facing the ski designer is to refine the ski's performance and to optimize its skiing characteristics in order to suit the needs of clearly defined skier groups. If one has the opportunity to test different models from the leading ski manufacturers, one will immediately notice how perfectly tailored the skis are to the requirements of certain skier groups. This is most obvious in the high-performance ski models, and this is where progress in design has been greatest. Especially in the high-performance area, the interrelationship between the design of new types of skis and the development of new skiing techniques is very clear. Modern turn techniques, like those for making carved turns on ice, would not have been possible without modern ski design.

The ski is the most important part of the ski–boot–binding system and therefore the major tool in the process that transfers steering impulses from the skier to the slope. The methods for applying steering forces to a ski (and the ability to do this) are different in different skier groups. For instance, an intermediate skier does not initiate a turn in the same way as an expert skier. For each skier group, ski models have been developed with skiing characteristics perfectly tuned to the ability level of the group. The designer creates the various skiing characteristics by combining different tech-

(*ABOVE*) The geometry of a ski. (*1*) Tip. (*2*) Shoulder. (*3*) Forward taper angle. (*4*) Side camber. (*5*) Waist. (*6*) Rear plow angle. (*7*) Heel. (*8*) Tail. (*9*) Shovel height. (*10*) Forward contact point. (*11*) Bottom camber. (*12*) Rear contact point. (*13*) Tail height.
(*BELOW*) The afterbody's side geometry has multiple functions. (**A**) When the ski runs in a straight course, it displaces snow on both sides of its afterbody. This causes lateral forces (*1* and *2*) to act on the ski. Since the direction of the ski coincides with its centerline (*3*), *1* and *2* cancel each other. (**B**) When you turn a ski, say, to the right, the lateral forces on the left-hand side increase while those on the right-

nical parameters, the most important of which are geometric features, elastic properties, inertia properties, and dynamic properties.

In this context it is important to note that a single parameter of a ski, isolated from the others, is meaningless to the skier. The final performance of any model is always the result of a combination of many parameters. It is possible to get identical skiing characteristics with different combinations of the separate features.

Geometric Features

A ski's geometry is one of the design features that contribute most to the skiing characteristics of the ski. Relatively small deviations from the proper side contour or from the ideal bottom-surface geometry will change those characteristics noticeably. Unfortunately, incorrect information on geometric features has been published repeatedly. The following should help the skier to acquire a knowledge of the proper terminology and thus to understand how the geometry of his ski contributes to its skiing characteristics.

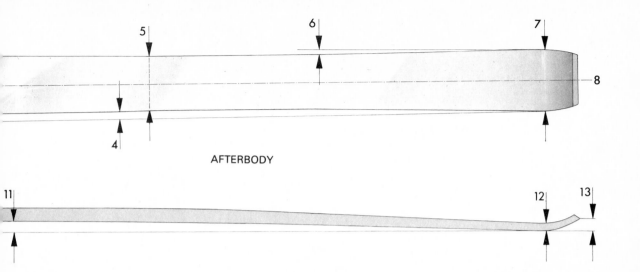

AFTERBODY

hand side decrease. The difference between them causes a turning moment that strives to return the ski to a straight course. This is called the stabilizing effect of the side geometry. The greater the rear plow angle, the stronger the stabilizing effect. Thus, the lateral stability is caused by the side geometry of the afterbody, not by the bottom groove. **(C)** When you set the ski on its right edge, force *1* no longer acts on the left-hand edge, whereas force *2* increases, causing the ski to turn to the right. The greater the rear taper angle, the greater this turning moment. Thus, skis with great side camber react to edging considerably faster than skis with little side camber.

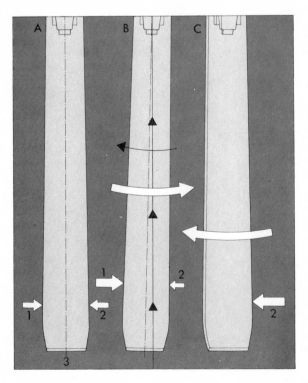

The Side Geometry

Side geometry, or side cut, can be defined as the configuration of the curve bordering the entire bottom surface of the ski. It differs greatly depending upon the ski's model group and manufacturer. All skis have in common the characteristic ski shape, which has the widest part in the shovel and the narrowest part of the running surface under the foot pad. From the narrowest part, called the waist, the edge follows a complicated curve, and the ski becomes wider toward the extremities. The shape of the curve and the amount of taper contribute greatly to the ski's performance. The size of the forward taper angle or the ratio between shoulder width and waist width affect the forgiveness of a ski (that is, its ability to reduce the effects of irregularities in the snow and of control actions made too forcefully by the skier) in schussing and in the transition period between two turns. The size of the forward taper angle and the ratio between shoulder width and waist width are not quite the same thing—the difference is too technical to go into here—but the effect is similar. In other words, the greater the width at the shovel in relation to the width at the waist, the less chance there is of catching an edge. The size of the rear plow angle or the ratio between heel width and waist width affect several other important skiing characteristics. The shape of the side cut in the afterbody affects how quickly a turn can be initiated and it governs lateral stability in schussing. Ski models that are skied very quickly from edge to edge are designed with emphasized plow angle, and this results in relatively great side cut.

A pronounced side cut has, however, some disadvantage in heavy snow. The increased "snow-plow" effect that it produces creates a higher snow-removement resistance. Because this may reduce speed on soft snow, high-speed skis (giant-slalom or downhill-racing skis) are designed with a "flat" side cut, that is, a small side camber and a small rear plow angle.

Bottom Camber

From what has just been said, we can conclude that the side geometry at the ski's extremities is of particularly great importance. The better a skier is, the more he uses the design features of the extremities of his skis. In order to make these design features work properly, the ski needs to be subjected to sufficient pressure at both ends. This is the main reason for the bottom camber, which is an arch of the bottom surface and is usually about 12 mm ($\frac{1}{2}$ inch) high. The amount of bottom camber is related to other characteristics. Stiff skis need less camber. Well-damped skis (which absorb vibrations quickly) are usually built with low camber.

The Geometry of the Running Surface

One of the usual methods of checking the quality of a ski is to make a line check, that is, an inspection of the longitudinal geometry of the running surfaces and of its conformity with the stiffness distribution. If such a conformity exists, the bottom surfaces of both skis will touch each other in a certain way when the skis are pressed together, as shown in the illustrations to the right. There must be no rolling contact from the extremities (that is, the size of the contact areas must not increase when the camber is decreased), and the travel of the contact points should be short. It is an advantage if there is a small gap between the running surfaces just behind the shovel contact point. Such a gap indicates a small camber and serves two purposes. Firstly, it ensures that sufficient pressure on the snow can be obtained at the contact points; this is a feature which is critical for steering maneuvers. Secondly, on "slow" snow, the mini-camber near the shovel breaks the surface tension of the hydro-mechanical gliding film between the running surface of the ski and the snow crystals, thus making faster skiing possible.

Another quality-ski feature which is very important is the proper lateral geometry of the running surfaces. A perfectly finished running surface—including the outermost surface of the steel edges—must be absolutely plane in the lateral direction. The lateral flatness of the ski can be

(ABOVE) A line check. When the skis are pressed together, the travel of the contact points (1, 2) should be short, as indicated on the two enlarged views of the shovels. A small gap (3) just behind the shovel contact point is an advantage. (4) Binding marks. The distance from the binding marks to your hands should be 10 cm (4 inches) on either side when you do a line check.
(ABOVE, FAR RIGHT) To check the bottom finish of a pair of skis, put the skis together, base to base, and look at them, either from behind (as here) or from in front. If the finish is perfect (1), there will be no gaps between the skis, whereas skis with a worn or wrong-

checked by means of a straight edge or by placing the skis on top of each other, running surface to running surface.

Elastic Properties

Besides the geometric design features, an essential part of a ski's performance depends on its elastic properties, that is, the ways in which the ski is deformed when subjected to the various forces encountered in skiing. As has been mentioned at the beginning of this chapter, the skier controls turns by varying the resistance forces acting on the steel edges of the skis. The contribution of the elastic properties to skiing performance is directly related to these resistance forces. The magnitude of the forces transmitted to the skier–ski system will determine its direction and velocity. At the same time, these forces cause the skis to deform, and this modifies the magnitude of the forces.

Because of the significant contribution of elastic properties to skiing characteristics, there are essential differences in flex between different ski models. These differences are best recognized by a look at the bending line, that is, the curve into which a ski bends when supported at the ends and weighted at the center. On an all-round ski model for intermediate skiers preferring moderate speed, the pressure is mainly distributed to the area close to the foot pad, while the ski's extremities are less loaded. Such a pressure distribution is advantageous for the stem-turn techniques and swiveled turns preferred by many intermediate skiers. On a high-performance ski model with so-called slalom characteristics, the pressure is distributed over a wider range. When turning on skis of this type, the skier utilizes the entire length of the edges. Skis with such a pressure distribution are best suited for precisely carved turns. The bending line also con-

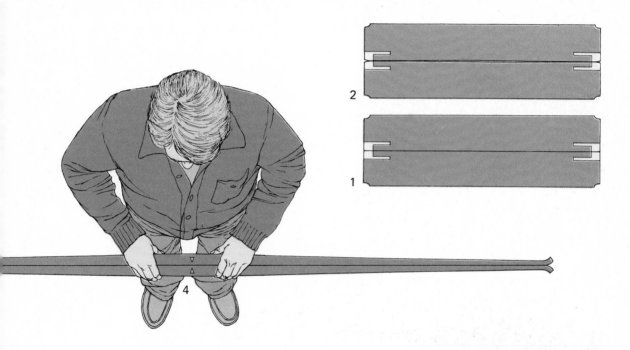

ly prepared finish (2) cannot be made to lie flush. Note that skis with perfect bottom finish should have deburred edges, since edges that are too sharp can cause trouble. Use fine abrasive paper to do this.

Around the shovels and the tail turn-ups, the steel edges must be dull. If they are not, bevel them with a file. The importance of

base finish is underlined by the fact that experienced service technicians are able to improve dramatically the performance characteristics of a ski merely by giving it a perfect base finish.

tributes to "snap," a positive force felt by the skier when a turn is released and the energy stored in the ski is returned. Good snap is a characteristic preferred by expert skiers. High-speed skis have a relatively soft shovel and forebody and a stiff middle and afterbody. The pressure distribution caused by such a bending line is most favorable for high-speed ski models, since it results in a low gliding resistance.

Generally, it might be said that a "soft" flex is desirable for most ski models. However, this can-

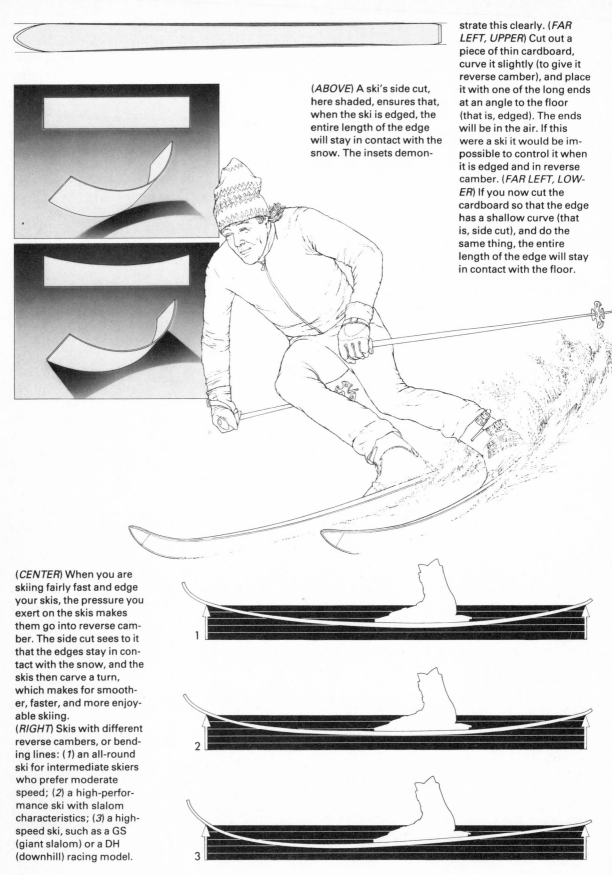

(*ABOVE*) A ski's side cut, here shaded, ensures that, when the ski is edged, the entire length of the edge will stay in contact with the snow. The insets demonstrate this clearly. (*FAR LEFT, UPPER*) Cut out a piece of thin cardboard, curve it slightly (to give it reverse camber), and place it with one of the long ends at an angle to the floor (that is, edged). The ends will be in the air. If this were a ski it would be impossible to control it when it is edged and in reverse camber. (*FAR LEFT, LOWER*) If you now cut the cardboard so that the edge has a shallow curve (that is, side cut), and do the same thing, the entire length of the edge will stay in contact with the floor.

(*CENTER*) When you are skiing fairly fast and edge your skis, the pressure you exert on the skis makes them go into reverse camber. The side cut sees to it that the edges stay in contact with the snow, and the skis then carve a turn, which makes for smoother, faster, and more enjoyable skiing.

(*RIGHT*) Skis with different reverse cambers, or bending lines: (*1*) an all-round ski for intermediate skiers who prefer moderate speed; (*2*) a high-performance ski with slalom characteristics; (*3*) a high-speed ski, such as a GS (giant slalom) or a DH (downhill) racing model.

not always be obtained. Metal skis, for instance, cannot be made with a soft flex for reasons of strength. Skis made from high-strength materials such as fiberglass, as well as skis with sufficient damping properties, can be designed to have a relatively soft flex.

When turning, a ski is not only subjected to bending but also to torsion. While the bending is distributed over the entire length of the ski, twisting occurs mainly at the shovel section when great forces act on the edge of the ski during turning or stopping maneuvers. The effect of torsional rigidity on the edge grip is a hobbyhorse with many ski experts, but extensive correlation studies have shown this effect to be overrated. Metal skis usually have great torsional rigidity, whereas box-construction fiberglass skis with continuous edges have moderate torsional rigidity. Fiberglass skis with cracked edges (that is, edges consisting of numerous small segments, which are joined by a small web of steel) and plastic top edges have relatively little torsional rigidity.

Inertia Properties

The inertia properties which are of interest to the skier are the ski's mass, which tells the skier how heavy a ski is, and the ski's moment of inertia (the swing weight), which is a measure of the ski's resistance to rotational acceleration. If two skis have equal but differently distributed mass, then the ski in which the mass is mainly concentrated to the foot-pad area has the lower moment of inertia.

Opinions differ among skiers as to the effects of mass and swing weight on skiing. Some skiers do not appreciate light-weight skis, whereas others—probably the larger group—consider light weight to be a most desirable ski feature. The reason opinions differ may well be a difference in skiing techniques. Skiers who stem prior to each turn, skiers who initiate turns with a heel push, and hot-doggers, in other words, all skiers whose skiing style requires sudden accelerations and decelerations by means of bodily forces will prefer light-weight skis. Skiers who tend to use the turning-aid features of the side cut as well as skiers who prefer to make fast, long-radius turns do not need light-weight skis—on the contrary. Such skiers ought to find that heavier skis contribute to better stability.

Dynamic Properties

A ski's dynamic properties are those characteristics which appear when the skier–ski system is in motion. Such properties are, of course, much more difficult to quantify than the geometrical or the elastic properties of a ski. One of the most important dynamic properties of a ski is its vibration characteristic, that is, its ability to absorb vibrations caused by irregularities in the terrain. Skis which are able to absorb vibrations quickly are said to be damped, whereas skis which are not able to do so are said to be vibratory.

When a vibratory ski carves a turn on an icy slope, forces of reaction act on the ski's loaded steel edge. If these forces act steadily and uniformly on the edge, the turn will be smooth and its course predictable. On soft, homogeneous snow, this is fairly easy, since the surface is uniform and the snow quickly damps any vibrations in the ski. Vibrations caused by irregularities on icy slopes, however, are not damped and may cause the ski's shoulder and heel areas to lose their edge bite. If this happens, the forces of reaction which are controlling the turn will no longer act on those sections of the ski. One way in which the edge bite—and, thus, the control over the ski—can be maintained in such a situation is to use skis with built-in damping characteristics. Well-damped skis with the proper flex distribution and side geometry tend to bite over their entire edge length on an icy slope. For those who have a carved-turn skiing style, this can be the best type of ski.

Well-damped skis are, however, not always desirable. Practical gliding tests have shown that controlled vibration in the ski is one of the best ways to generate an advantageous hydromechanical gliding film between the running surface of the ski and the snow crystals. Thus, high-speed skis should preferably be highly vibratory.

It is, of course, not easy to select skis on the basis of this information only. A general rule, however, is that metal does not have the capacity to absorb vibrations; plastics and wood do. Metal or fiberglass skis with continuous steel edges and metal top edges are vibratory and are therefore best for high-speed skiing. Fiberglass skis with cracked edges are usually well damped and are thus best for carved-turn skiing on icy slopes.

Modern Ski Constructions

Today's ski constructions are true masterpieces of modern technology, and ski manufacturers must use sophisticated materials, complicated production methods, and stringent quality control in order to meet the high standards now demanded by skiers. In their efforts to find the best materials, the manufacturers have tried out almost every advanced, high-strength material available.

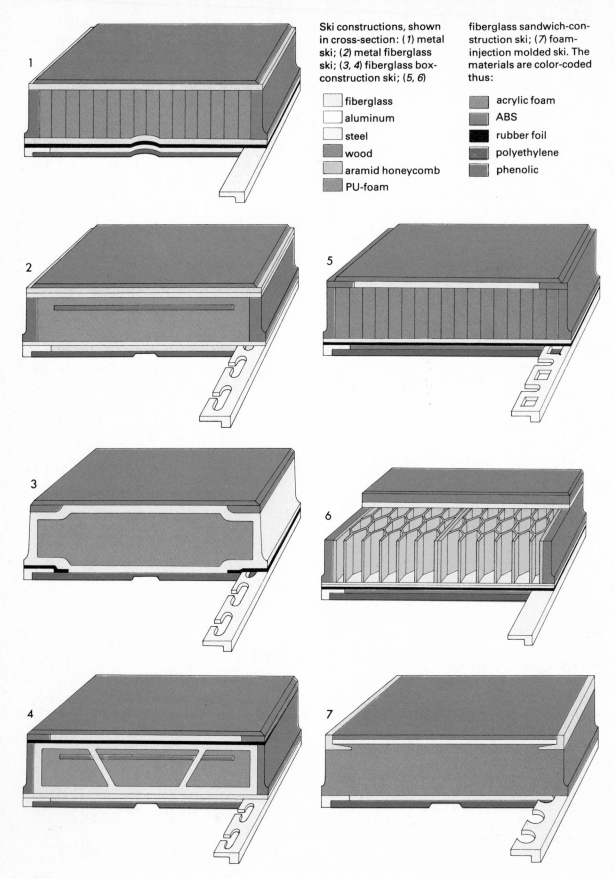

Ski constructions, shown in cross-section: (1) metal ski; (2) metal fiberglass ski; (3, 4) fiberglass box-construction ski; (5, 6) fiberglass sandwich-construction ski; (7) foam-injection molded ski. The materials are color-coded thus:

- fiberglass
- aluminum
- steel
- wood
- aramid honeycomb
- PU-foam
- acrylic foam
- ABS
- rubber foil
- polyethylene
- phenolic

The immense choice of brands and designs on the market at present is confusing for all skiers, even the experts, and this chapter could not possibly cover even a small part of what is available. The following presentation concentrates therefore on the "classic" ski designs.

Metal skis are usually sandwich constructions, that is, composite structures in which a low-strength core is reinforced on both sides with layers of stiff, high-strength metal (aluminum). The "classic" metal ski was introduced in 1950 by an American, Howard Head, founder of the Head Ski Company, and later improved by the Fischer company in Austria. It still holds a considerable market share. Typical for the metal ski is that it has great torsional rigidity, is vibratory, may have insufficient bending strength if designed with soft flex, and is simple to produce.

Metal fiberglass skis represent a subsequent development of the "classic" metal ski. The addition of fiberglass laminates to the aluminum layers change the metal ski's characteristics. The bending strength of metal fiberglass skis is greater than that of metal skis; they are vibratory and have great torsional rigidity.

Fiberglass box construction skis. A box construction is a composite structure in which the load-bearing member consists of webs and flanges, arranged in "box" form; sometimes the "box" is also reinforced internally by cross-webs. Skis of the fiberglass box-construction type are usually manufactured according to the wet-wrap process, the fiberglass being cured in the ski mold. The wet-wrapped box can also be combined with pre-cured fiberglass or metal layers. Fiberglass box-construction skis are usually well damped, have great torsional rigidity and high bending strength.

Fiberglass sandwich-construction skis are made from pre-cured, unidirectional fiberglass laminates which can be combined with any type of core material and any type of steel edge and top edge. All parts of the ski are usually assembled and bonded in a single operation. Since the dimensions and the mechanical properties of all parts of the ski can be maintained within a narrow tolerance range, the same is true for the physical properties of the finished skis. Fiberglass sandwich-construction skis have a very high bending strength, and they are sufficiently damped to have good carving characteristics on icy slopes. The range of possible flex and torsional characteristics is wide.

Foam-injection-molded skis are made from pre-assembled top and bottom layers; these are placed in a mold which is then closed. Liquid polyurethan containing an expanding agent is then injected into the mold between the top and bottom layers. As the foam expands and sets, it bonds the parts and forms the core of the ski. Foam-injection-molded skis are simple to produce but have a limited bending strength. The method is frequently used for low-cost skis.

Selecting the Proper Ski Model

To the quality-minded buyer unfamiliar with the latest market offerings, shopping for skis can be a confusing experience. However, if you follow a few basic rules, the chances of ending up with the wrong skis will be reduced. Always seek the advice of an expert; once again, the trained sales staff of a specialized ski shop is the best source of expertise.

The ski shop will already have made a preliminary selection from the immense amount of models on the market, so there will only be a reasonable range on display. As the salesman is trained and is familiar with the performance characteristics of the various models, he can recommend skis that best suit your needs. First of all, however, he will ask you some questions in order to establish your "skier profile." What is your performance level? Do you ski often? What type of terrain do you like? What speed do you prefer? He can then relate your skier profile to one of the skier target groups defined by the manufacturers. (Almost all man-

Ski length groups. (*1*) A full-length ski is twelve or more percent longer than the skier is tall. (*2*) A mid-length ski is equally long as or up to twelve percent longer than the skier is tall. (*3*) A short ski is shorter than the skier is tall.

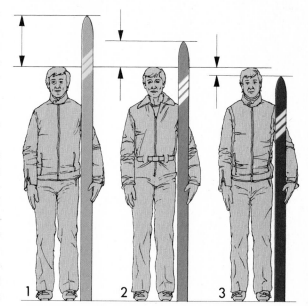

ufacturers place their ski models in clearly defined groups that relate to the proficiency of the skiers.) The skier target groups are:

1 Novice through intermediate group (weekend recreational skiers who prefer moderate speed on gentle terrain).

2 Sport group (advanced through expert skiers; able to master all kinds of terrain at moderate to high speeds).

3 High-performance group (expert skiers through top competitors; able to master the most difficult terrain at high speed).

4 Specialty group (those who indulge in the types of skiing that are not mentioned above, such as ballet, ski touring in high mountain areas, and so on.

Once you have related your skier profile to one of these groups, it will be easier for you to select a suitable ski model. However, this does not automatically guarantee that you pick the ski that suits you best, because within each group there are numerous variations. For instance, skiers in the sport group can choose a model that is well suited to icy conditions, or a model suited to soft snow. In the high-performance group models may have SL-characteristics (for short-radius turns) or GS-characteristics (for long-radius turns—cruising skis). SL stands for slalom, and GS for giant slalom. By studying the manufacturer's model chart and conferring with the salesmen, you ought to be able to pick the skis that suit you best.

It is very important to follow the manufacturer's length recommendations. These vary from model to model. Each model usually belongs to one of the three length groups: full length, mid length, and short ski (see illustration on p. 37).

To sum up, we can say that the basic steps to be taken in selecting skis are:

1 Establish your skier profile and relate it to the corresponding skier group.

2 Correlate this skier group with the corresponding ski model group.

3 Study the model variation within this group and select the model that suits the way you want to ski, the surface on which you want to ski, etc.

4 Select the right size by referring to the length recommendations of the manufacturer.

Finally, a few words of warning to help you to avoid some very common mistakes:

1 Be realistic in determining your skier profile.

2 Be suspicious of manufacturers' superlatives. There is no ski that can do "just everything."

3 Don't waste time discussing individual features, such as torsion, damping, materials configura-

tions, etc. What is important to you is the final result—the ski's performance on the slope.

4 Don't be impressed by facts that will have no effect whatsoever on your skiing, for instance the racing success of a particular model or brand. Olympic champions use specially made skis that have little in common with the ski you ought to have. Details such as care-intensive racing bases may be very important to a World Cup racer, but they are not necessarily of any advantage to you.

Maintenance

Alpine skis usually come in for a lot of heavy wear and tear, not so much to the structure of the skis but rather to the sensitive base materials and to the steel edges. After only two days' skiing, a skier can feel the difference in the way the edges bite. Oxidation on the bases (caused by road salt, for instance) and other defects in the running-surface material make the skis slow and difficult to handle. If you don't take care of your skis, you will lose a lot of the enjoyment of skiing.

Remember the following rules:

1 Frequent filing or sanding of the steel edges will ensure good turning performance on hard slopes.

2 Maintenance of the base material and frequent waxing will ensure a good gliding base that will make for easier turning.

3 Clean and dry your skis after each day's skiing. Store the skis in a dry place.

4 Protect the running surfaces of the skis when transporting them by strapping them together, running surfaces face to face, with safety straps. Place the skis in a ski bag. Even if the skis are to be

Base and edge maintenance. (*1*) Dry the base and clean it with acetone or wax remover. (*2*) To repair gouges, light a P-tex candle and fill all the gouges amply with the melted polyethylene. Allow to cool. (*3*) Trim the repaired areas flush with the base, using a scraper held in both hands. (*4*) Flat-file the base, using a magicut file, if the skis are heavily worn, or a 30-cm (12 inches) mill bastard file, if the skis are only lightly worn. (*5*) Check the flatness of the base with a straight edge. (*6*) Side-file the ski, using a mill bastard file. File only in one direction, making certain that the edge is square. (*7*) Remove any burrs that have formed from filing. Use an emery cloth or a pocket stone held against the steel edge. (*8*) Warm a bar of wax by holding it briefly against an iron set at "wool," then rub the bar of wax against the ski base. Repeat until the whole base is covered by a layer of wax. Now, "iron" the base, working your way down it as the wax melts. (*9*) Scrape any excess wax from the base, leaving only a thin coat. Remove all wax from the sides and steel edges of the ski. (*10*) Buff the wax, using a clean cloth.

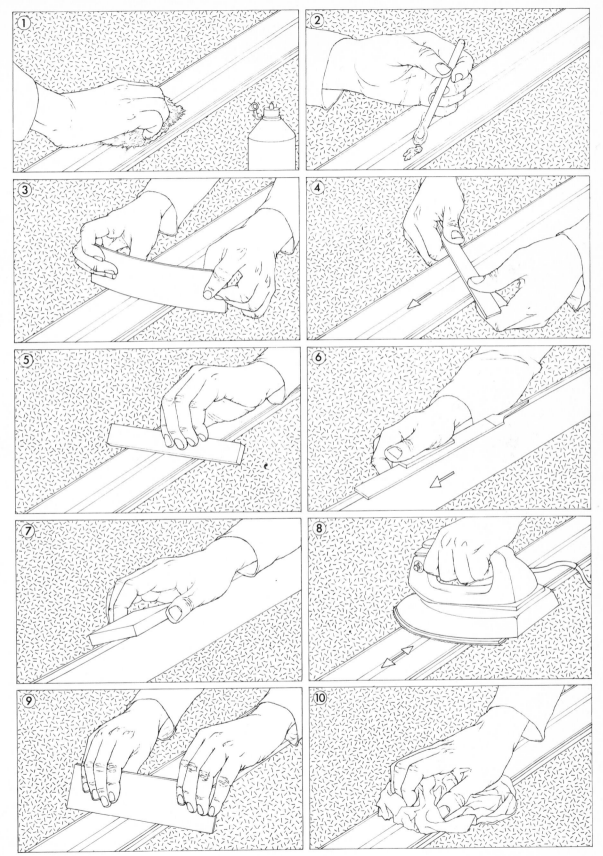

carried on the roof of an automobile, it is advisable to use a ski bag or, at the very least, to protect the bindings with plastic covers. Many airlines provide plastic ski bags for those of their passengers who do not have bags of their own.

The Alpine Ski Boot

Some experts consider the ski boot the most important piece of skiing equipment, and there is some truth in this. Without playing down the importance of the ski, we can state that even the best ski will not perform well if matched with an ill-suited boot. The realization of this fact has caused a tremendous technological revolution in the design of ski boots. The last two decades have seen the boot change completely. In the past, the ski boot was primarily made for walking. Its main function was to keep the foot warm and dry; no safety-related and very few performance-related demands were made on the boot. Progress in ski boot design appears all the more dramatic because the most important advances took place in less than one decade, while similar advances in ski development were spread over three decades.

The Boot's Role in the Ski–Boot–Binding System

As already mentioned, all skiing maneuvers are carried out and controlled by varying the resistance forces that act on the bottom edge, or running surface, of the ski. The skier varies these forces by

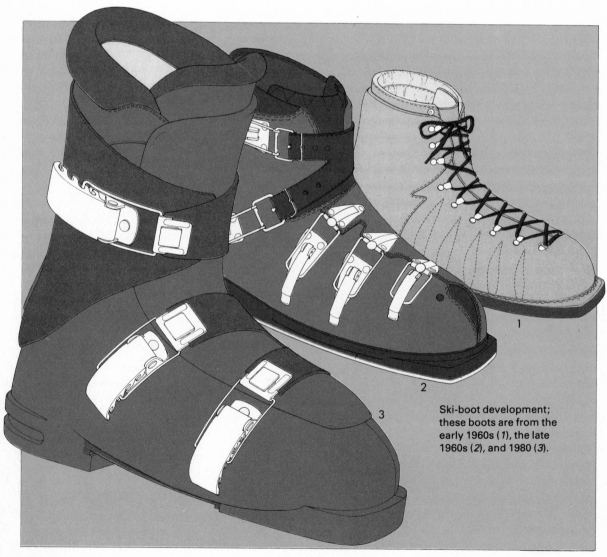

Ski-boot development; these boots are from the early 1960s (*1*), the late 1960s (*2*), and 1980 (*3*).

changing the load applied and by shifting his weight in the longitudinal direction. The boots are his means of communication with his skis; if subtle changes of weight distribution are not faithfully transmitted by the boot to the ski, the skier's efforts will be ineffective. Ski boots can make or break a skier's performance, for whatever he does with his skis must be done via his boots. They are the distribution centers of all the steering forces and the sensitive transducers of all the control impulses produced by the skier.

In order to distribute the steering forces properly, the boot must fill the following six requirements, the first two of which are performance-related, the next two are comfort-related, and the final two are safety-related.

1 It must be designed in accordance with the principles of applied biomechanics and foot anatomy.
2 It must produce a tight and sensitive joint to the muscles of the foot and lower leg.
3 The inside of the boot must be soft and resilient to avoid the creation of painful pressure spots.
4 The boot must keep the foot warm and allow sufficient blood circulation.
5 The interface dimensions of the boot sole, that is, the dimensions of those parts of the boot sole that meet with the binding when connected for functional use, must meet the requirements of international safety standards.
6 The sole must be designed to allow safe walking on slippery terrain.

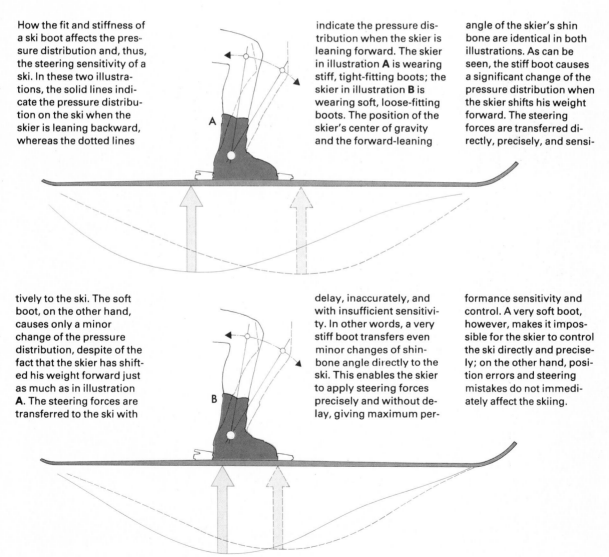

How the fit and stiffness of a ski boot affects the pressure distribution and, thus, the steering sensitivity of a ski. In these two illustrations, the solid lines indicate the pressure distribution on the ski when the skier is leaning backward, whereas the dotted lines indicate the pressure distribution when the skier is leaning forward. The skier in illustration **A** is wearing stiff, tight-fitting boots; the skier in illustration **B** is wearing soft, loose-fitting boots. The position of the skier's center of gravity and the forward-leaning angle of the skier's shin bone are identical in both illustrations. As can be seen, the stiff boot causes a significant change of the pressure distribution when the skier shifts his weight forward. The steering forces are transferred directly, precisely, and sensitively to the ski. The soft boot, on the other hand, causes only a minor change of the pressure distribution, despite of the fact that the skier has shifted his weight forward just as much as in illustration **A**. The steering forces are transferred to the ski with delay, inaccurately, and with insufficient sensitivity. In other words, a very stiff boot transfers even minor changes of shinbone angle directly to the ski. This enables the skier to apply steering forces precisely and without delay, giving maximum performance sensitivity and control. A very soft boot, however, makes it impossible for the skier to control the ski directly and precisely; on the other hand, position errors and steering mistakes do not immediately affect the skiing.

Stiffness is not the only important feature of a ski boot, and a modern boot contains a complicated mechanism which enables it to perform as a sensitive transducer of steering forces. To start with, the ski boot must provide an anatomically correct adjustment of the shin-bone angle. This requirement is best met by a two-piece shell design, where the upper shell (1) is joined to the lower shell (2) by means of a low-friction hinge (3) at the ankle joint. The upper shell must be set at an angle (4) which corresponds to the "natural" position of a skier of the performance group for which the boot is intended. On many high-performance boot models, this angle can be adjusted to the individual preference of the skier. When this is

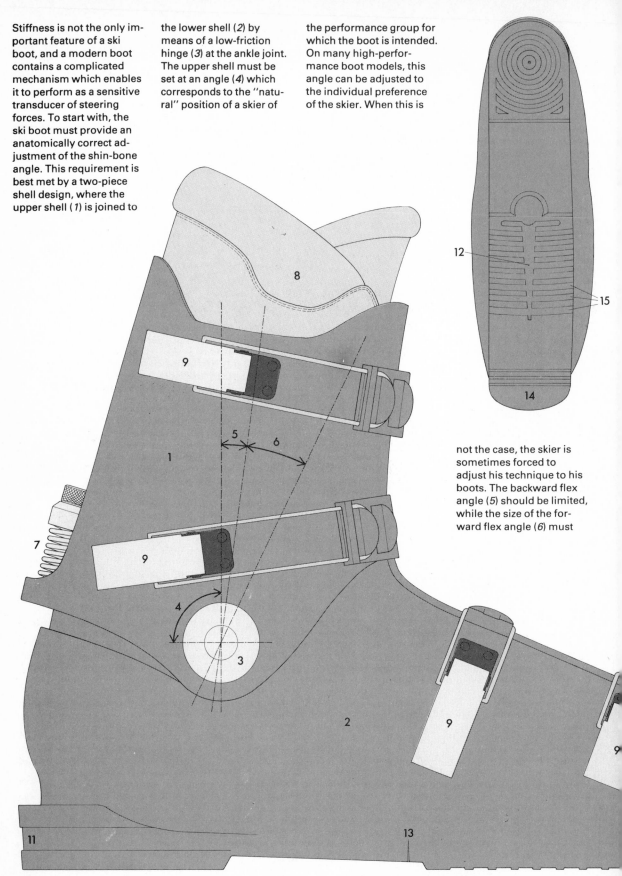

not the case, the skier is sometimes forced to adjust his technique to his boots. The backward flex angle (5) should be limited, while the size of the forward flex angle (6) must

42

correspond to the performance profile of the target group. The boot's forward flex behavior, that is, the motion of the upper shell from 4 to the forward-lean position, must be controlled by a progressively increasing resistance. On simple, low-performance boots, the forward flex behavior is controlled by the stiffness of the shell material or by the friction between the upper and lower shells. A stiff upper shell provides a small forward flex angle or a rather rapid increase in resistance. Since the stiffness of plastics varies with temperature, boot designers try to keep the forward flex independent of the boot material by incorporating elastic elements. These may consist of steel compression springs (7) or of rubber blocks and are exchangeable, so that the resistance can be adjusted.

The inner boot (8) must fulfil the following requirements: It must fit the foot so perfectly that, even if the boot should be buckled almost tightly enough to stop the blood from circulating in the foot, no painful pressure points should

be felt. A particularly good fit is needed at the heel, while the toes should be able to move freely. The padding should not be too thick, since all steering forces must be transmitted directly and without delay. It should be removable from the boot, since it can then easily be cleaned and dried. A removable inner boot further provides possibilities to make the boot fit optimally by means of additional padding or corrective grinding.

The boot's closure system must have functional, correctly located buckles (9). High-performance boots are still designed with three or four buckles in order to ensure a perfect fit. Low-performance boots usually have fewer buckles. On quality boots, the buckle tension can be adjusted to allow for varying conditions.

The sole of the boot is attached to the ski by means of the holding devices of the binding. If a plate binding is used, the effect of the boot-sole's shape on the safety functions of the binding is insignificant, but if a heel-and-toe-unit binding is used, the release mechanism's function to a large extent depends on the shape of the boot's sole. The shape of the soles in areas 10 and 11 must be designed in accordance with the safety standards to ensure the safe function of the release binding's toe and heel units. Area 12 is the friction surface which meets the antifriction pad of the binding. The condition of this friction area is vital for the proper function of the release binding. The boot-sole midpoint mark (13) is an index point for determining the proper location of the boot on the ski. The beveled area (14) and the recesses (15) contribute to the skier's safety when he walks in slippery terrain.

As some of the requirements in this considerable list contradict others, certain conflicts arise. For instance, the performance-related requirements are often fulfilled only at the expense of comfort, and vice versa. The outcome of these conflicts is that the ski boot's design is a compromise between the requirements of performance and comfort. This is hardly noticeable today, as boots are of such excellent quality and offer the maximum of performance and a high degree of comfort. Thankfully, it is now unnecessary to suffer pain in the pursuit of top performance. Skiing with aching feet cannot be good skiing. The main problem as regards boot comfort is not one of design or material, but rather one of the non-standardization of human feet. However, since the lasts of the manufacturers differ from each other, it ought to be possible for every skier to find a well-fitting boot. Only if you have a very unusual foot shape is a specially made boot to be recommended.

Recommendations for Proper Boot Selection

Basically the same recommendations as those given for selecting skis apply when selecting boots. Many skiers unfortunately make mistakes when choosing boots, and thus miss many of the advantages offered by today's modern boot designs. The following are the rules when buying boots:

1 Buy only from a dealer who carries high-quality merchandise and a large stock of brands and models.

2 Take your time when shopping around. Visit several shops and look at the different brands. If you avoid the rush hour, the salesman will have enough time to give you proper service.

3 Pick a boot model with a performance profile that corresponds to the performance profile of your ski. Many boot manufacturers group their models in performance categories that are similar to those given to alpine skis (intermediate, sport, high performance, racing), and this makes it relatively easy to coordinate ski and boot.

4 A frequent mistake made is to select too big a boot. It is much better to pick a very tight boot and to reshape the shell or inner boot at probable pressure points, than to take a larger size in order to avoid a single pressure point. Plastic shells can be reshaped with a hot-air blower and reshaping tools. A good shop will be well equipped with such tools. Remember that fitting takes time, so you should buy and fit your boots during the "quiet"

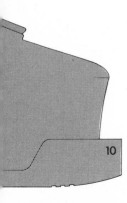

10

To try on a pair of boots. Take the inner boots out of the shells. (*1*) Stand up in the bare shells with your toes just touching the fronts of the shells. (*2*) You should now be able to look down the back of each heel and see no less than 10 mm ($\frac{1}{2}$ inch) and no more than 20 mm ($\frac{7}{8}$ inch) clearance between your heels and the shells (to allow for toe clearance, padding, and insulation after the feet have adapted and molded the inner boot).

(*3*) To check width, pull your toes back so that your feet are where they would be if you had the inner boots on. The widest part of your

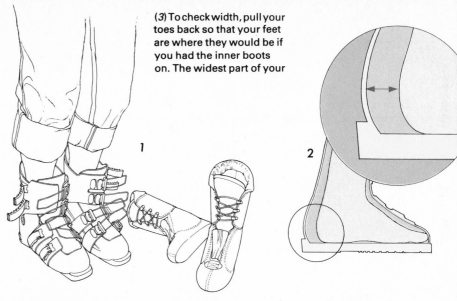

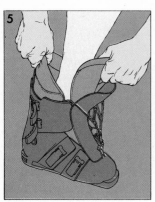
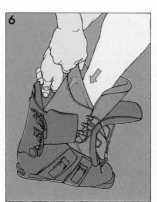

shell, still pulling on the inner boot. This sets your heel into the heel of both the inner boot and the shell. (*9*) Close the buckle closest to your instep first, to ensure that instep and heel are pushed back. (*10*) Flex against this buckle to drive the heel back. (*11*) Close the top buckle. This enables you to close the instep buckle tighter. (*12*) Close the two forefoot buckles last. The boots should now feel tight all round your feet. Your toes should touch the fronts when you stand up; when you flex forward, they should be hardly touching the fronts. Keep the boots on for ten minutes or so, flexing hard and walking about. The

inner boots' materials will begin to adapt to your feet and to the shells' cavities. Your heels will move back slowly, relieving the pressure on your toes. After two days' skiing, the boots will feel bigger and your toes will no longer touch their fronts.

shopping hours. Like top-class skiers, beginners and intermediate skiers should give priority to fit, not comfort, because if the boot fits too loosely, the learning process will be slowed down. The loss of forgiveness resulting from a tighter boot is more than compensated by the increased sensitivity of edge feel and by the ease with which more precisely carved turns can be made. Another important thing to remember is that you ought to stand flat on the skis, not on the inside or outside edges. This is difficult for those who are bowlegged or knock-kneed, as they cannot stand flat. While this is not a serious problem, you ought to remedy it if you are interested in improving your skiing. A doctor or a good ski shop can arrange an insole which will enable you to put your boot flat on the ground. Ski shops are normally equipped with measuring equipment which will indicate how many degrees you are off a regular flat stance, and they can insert suitable cant plates under the bindings, and this will make the skis lie completely flat

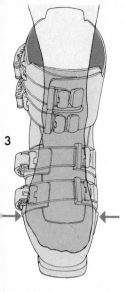

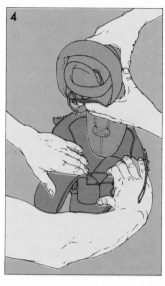

feet should now just touch the shell. (*4*) Insert the inner boots so that there are no folds or wrinkles. Get someone to help you. For fitting and for the first days of skiing, wear only thin nylon or silk socks. Pull up on the inner boot and tongue as you put the boot on. (*5*) To insert your foot easily into a conventional, four-buckle boot, spread the flaps slightly, position the tongue against the outside of the flap, and use the tongue as a guide for the foot to slide into the boot. (*6*) If it is hard to slide the foot down into the boot, pull the inner boot half out of the shell. Press your heel into the inner boot's heel and push both down into the shell's heel. (*7*) Grasp the back of the inner boot with one hand and push the shell down with the other. Pull the inner boot up about 10 cm (4 inches), lifting your heel and flexing your knee. (*8*) Push your heel down firmly to the rear of the

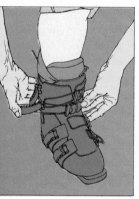

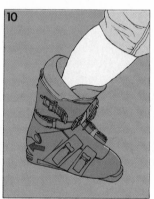

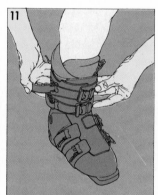

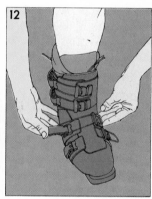

(*BELOW*) If you are knock-kneed (*1*) or bowlegged (*2*), you will not be able to hold your boots flat on the skis. Special insoles (*3, 4*) can be used to correct this. Cant plates have the same effect but are inserted under the bindings.

on the ground. Cant plates are very common and help many skiers to avoid catching the edges when parallel turning and also enables them to ride a flat ski downhill instead of skiing on the edge.

Care of Ski Boots

1 Keep the friction area of the boot sole clean and smooth.

2 Remove the inner boot after skiing. Dry the liner and the inner cavity shell. Buckle the outer-boot shell to keep the shape.

3 If the forward flex behavior is controlled by friction, lubricate the friction surfaces with waterproof, silicone-type lubricant.

4 Before going skiing, make sure that the boot is warm. Keep it indoors overnight, never in the trunk of your automobile. Remember, however, that too warm a boot can cause condensation problems.

5 Your skiing boots are not walking shoes, so don't walk around in them, especially not on gravel or asphalt.

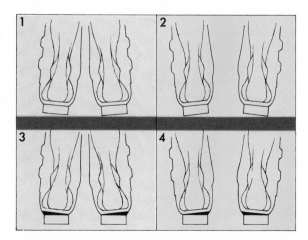

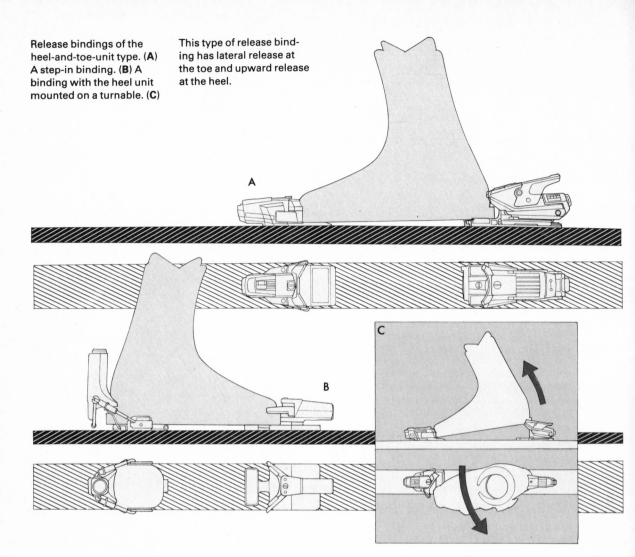

Release bindings of the heel-and-toe-unit type. (**A**) A step-in binding. (**B**) A binding with the heel unit mounted on a turnable. (**C**) This type of release binding has lateral release at the toe and upward release at the heel.

The Release Binding

The boot + ski system is complemented by the binding, which acts as the link between the two elements. The performance-related characteristics of the skis and boots are the most important to the skier, but as far as the bindings are concerned, the important features are the safety-related ones.

The purpose of a release binding is to retain the boot on the ski and to release the boot from the ski whenever necessary. The release binding must provide a reliable coupling that keeps the skier's foot attached to the ski despite the bumps, shocks, and other forces encountered in normal skiing. The skier must be able to rely on the release binding to release his foot from the ski before the forces generated on the ski can be transmitted to the lower leg, if those forces are great enough to cause injury.

Binding Design Requirements

A well-designed binding must release instantly when necessary, but it must also be able to absorb shocks without releasing. Shocks are quite common in alpine skiing and are generally not dangerous. However, a binding that opens too early or too easily is as dangerous as a binding that does not open at all. Due to their mass, the skier's boot and leg provide a significant resistance to sudden acceleration. If the coupling between the boot and the ski is very rigid, the binding's release mechanism will sense any impact immediately. A more elastic coupling can reduce the magnitude of the impact sensed by the release mechanism and lengthen the time in which it is felt. All anti-shock mechanisms are based on this elasticity. The lateral elasticity of the toe-piece allows the boot to return instantaneously to its centered position after the shock has been absorbed by the ski.

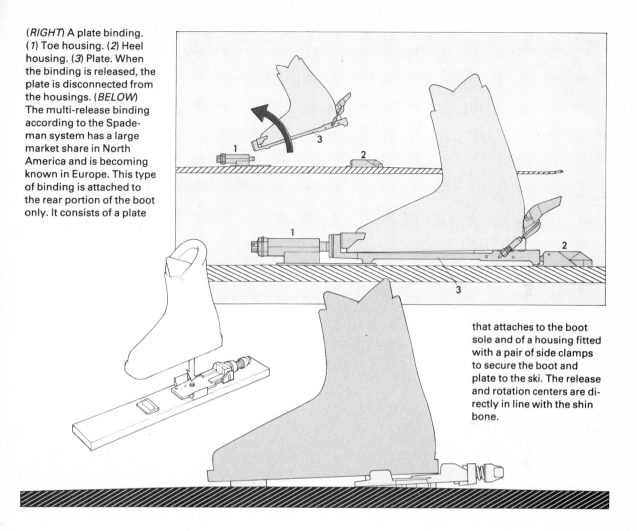

(*RIGHT*) A plate binding. (*1*) Toe housing. (*2*) Heel housing. (*3*) Plate. When the binding is released, the plate is disconnected from the housings. (*BELOW*) The multi-release binding according to the Spademan system has a large market share in North America and is becoming known in Europe. This type of binding is attached to the rear portion of the boot only. It consists of a plate that attaches to the boot sole and of a housing fitted with a pair of side clamps to secure the boot and plate to the ski. The release and rotation centers are directly in line with the shin bone.

The vertical elasticity of the heel-piece allows overloads caused by skiing errors to be absorbed. The longitudinal elasticity ensures that the boot applies sufficient pressure on the toe-piece and increases the ability of the binding system to absorb the flexing of the ski.

Friction occurs where the boot meets the ski and between any surfaces of the binding that must slide against each other. A properly designed binding will control the friction between the boot and the binding and inside the binding. Nowadays, manufacturers use several devices to control the friction occurring at all the interfaces. Antifriction rollers, for instance, have been fitted inside the toe-piece to make release predictable and to make the boot return more quickly to the center position. The anti-friction pad of the toe-piece, by many skiers wrongly considered to be an insignificant part of the binding, is instead an important con-tributor to the reliability and proper function of the binding.

Most release bindings used in Europe today are of the heel-and-toe-unit type; in North America, the market is shared with several plate-binding systems.

Heel-and-Toe-Unit Systems

There are two versions of this type of release binding. One is commonly called a step-in binding and consists of separate toe- and heel-pieces. The other has a heel-piece mounted on a turntable. The advantage of this latter system is that the axis of rotation coincides with the shin bone's axis in the case of a twist release.

Plate-Binding Systems

A plate binding consists of three elements: a toe housing, a heel housing, and a plate that can be attached to the sole of the boot. In the process of release the boot sole is not released from the binding, as in the previous system, but the plate is disconnected from the housings. This means that the plate binding is independent of the shape and quality of the boot sole. Changes in the boot sole, caused by wear, dirt, or changes of temperature, do not influence the release process. Plate bindings release in several directions, both at the heel and at the toe.

When Buying Bindings

1 Don't look for a bargain. The difference in price between a poor and a top-quality binding is insignificant when compared to the cost of an injury.
2 Preferably, you should look for bindings that have been approved by official consumer organizations (IAS in Germany, BfU in Switzerland). A certificate from such an organization guarantees that the binding meets international safety standards.
3 Some boots do not work with some bindings, so

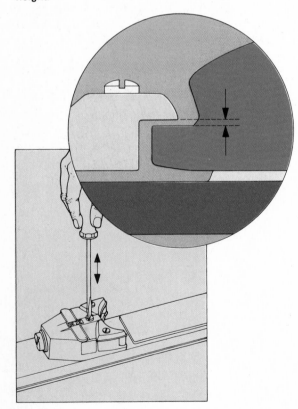

Adjusting the toe-cup height. The screw at the top of the toe-piece is used to increase or decrease the height.

bring your boot along when you are buying a new binding.
4 Buy the binding from a certified dealer who has the necessary expertise to mount, adjust, and maintain the bindings properly.

To Mount a Binding Properly

Mounting and adjusting release bindings is a skilled job that should be carried out with great care. Technically superior work can be done best in a shop that has the necessary expertise and tools. If for some reason you are going to mount the binding yourself, follow these rules:
1 The binding must be positioned so that the midpoint mark on the sole of the boot lines up with the line inscribed on the side wall or top surface of the ski. Should your ski not have a boot-sole midpoint mark, you can find the mark in the following way. Find the midpoint of the ski's chord length (the straight line distance along the ski's center line, between the tail and the tip). Measure 155 mm (6.1 inches) from there toward the tail. This point is the boot-sole midpoint on the ski.
2 The binding should be mounted on the center-line of the ski. Even if your boot has been asymmetrically designed, it is intended to work with symmetrically mounted bindings.
3 Drill holes in the ski according to the manufacturer's instructions. If no instructions are available, use a drill diameter of 4.0 mm (0.16 inches) and a drill hole depth of 9.0 mm (0.35 inches).
4 Tapping improves the retention strength of the screws. (A tap is a tool that cuts a thread in the wall of the drill hole.) The screwdriver bit should be cross recess—Pozidrive No. 3.

To Adjust Bindings

1 Adjust the toe-cup height to the upper surface of the boot sole. Most bindings work best with a 1-mm (0.04 inches) clearance between boot sole and antifriction pad. Too much clearance may have a bad effect on edge control. Too little may hinder lateral release.
2 On some bindings, the heel-cup height must be adjusted to avoid premature release.
3 Adjust the forward pressure in accordance with the manufacturer's instructions. Most heel-pieces have some kind of an indicator for this, and it should align with an index mark on the heel track when the boot is in the binding.
4 If you have a plate binding, take care that the distance between the toe housing and the heel housing is the correct one. Too great a distance has the same effect as insufficient forward pressure in

a toe-heel binding, and this may have a critical effect on the release function.

The Binding's Release Setting

Purchasing an expensive binding and mounting it properly does not automatically guarantee protection from leg injury. Statistics of skiing injuries indicate that not every skier who uses a modern release binding avails himself of its advantages. The reason for this is not inadequate equipment, but rather improper setting. Skiers' ignorance of how to set, maintain, and change a release setting is the true cause of many leg injuries.

The following rules are, therefore, important:

1 There is no such thing as a totally safe release binding system. However, the protection provided by a properly installed release binding is sufficient to guard against injury in a "normal" fall.

2 Safe limits for each individual skier's release settings can be determined and are based on scientific studies made on the resistance of bone and ligament to breakage. In Europe the Tibia Size Method, which is based on IAS recommendations, is used. In the United States the Weight and Ability Method, which is based on the Lipe system, is used. The two methods differ only slightly.

3 In all countries where alpine skiing is a common sport, technical committees have been set up to form standards for release settings on bindings. In some European countries, safety standards have already been established and can be enforced by law. In the United States, the ASTM committee F-8 on Sports Equipment has proposed a "Practice for procedure for functional tests and adjustments of bindings." This document provides guidelines for testing the functions and release mechanism of the ski + boot + binding system.

4 To set a binding and to test its release mechanism is complicated. Release tests must be performed with sophisticated instruments that indicate the force, torque, or moment applied. There-

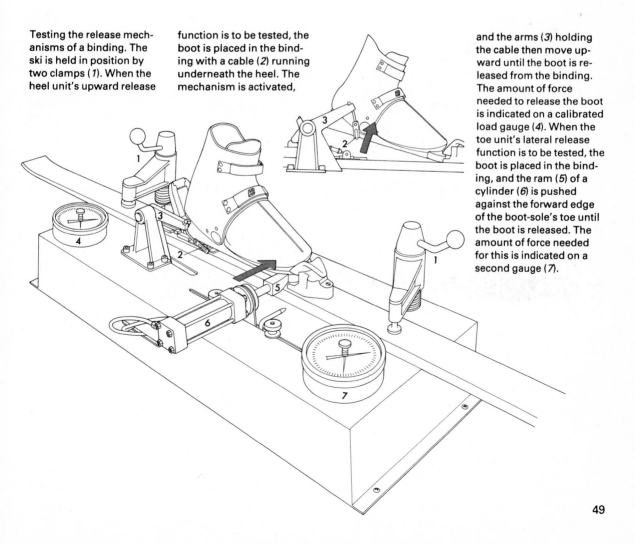

Testing the release mechanisms of a binding. The ski is held in position by two clamps (*1*). When the heel unit's upward release function is to be tested, the boot is placed in the binding with a cable (*2*) running underneath the heel. The mechanism is activated, and the arms (*3*) holding the cable then move upward until the boot is released from the binding. The amount of force needed to release the boot is indicated on a calibrated load gauge (*4*). When the toe unit's lateral release function is to be tested, the boot is placed in the binding, and the ram (*5*) of a cylinder (*6*) is pushed against the forward edge of the boot-sole's toe until the boot is released. The amount of force needed for this is indicated on a second gauge (*7*).

fore only a well-equipped ski shop can make such a test. Don't trust guesswork—use the best expertise available.

The release mechanisms should be checked on the following occasions:

1 At the beginning of each season.
2 When you replace your boots.
3 When you have let someone else use your skis.
4 When your bindings have been repaired or altered in any way, for instance by the addition of a ski stopper or a new antifriction pad.

Binding Maintenance

1 Keep your bindings free from road salt and grime. Protect them with plastic covers or—preferably—use ski bags when transporting your skis.
2 Pay attention to the surface of the antifriction pad. Friction rapidly increases when the antifriction pad gets dirty or worn. Replace the pad if its surface is in bad condition.
3 Inspect and lubricate your bindings two or three times a season in order to avoid unpleasant surprises.

Ski Retention Devices

The purpose of ski retention devices, such as safety straps or ski brakes, is to keep the skis close to a falling skier after the bindings have been released. This prevents the skier himself and other skiers from being injured by runaway skis, and the skier can easily retrieve his skis afterwards.

With the advent of release bindings, accidents caused by runaway skis increased greatly. A ski hurtling down a slope on its own accelerates to a tremendous speed and may cause serious injuries to anyone hit by it. The obvious solution to this problem is to keep the ski attached to the skier. This is done with safety straps, which are simply attached to the boot and to a part of the binding which cannot come apart from the ski.

In recent years, the ability of safety straps to prevent injuries caused by released skis has been questioned. In an informal report, submitted to the ASTM skiing safety committee by Dr L. Young (MIT) in 1978, it was indicated that approximately ten percent of all skiing injuries could be attributed to flailing skis, which had been attached to the skier by means of a safety strap. Flailing skis can cause head injuries, bruises, and lacerations.

The solution to this problem is to use ski brakes

instead of safety straps. A ski brake is a device which should preferably be integrated with the ski's release binding and which is designed to slow down and stop a ski when its binding has been released and the ski is in contact with the snow. As a number of skiing injury statistics indicate, the use of ski brakes provides a solution to most of the problems caused by runaway skis.

We therefore recommend ski brakes for recreational and high-performance (racing) skiers alike. Such brakes offer the best possibility to avoid self-inflicted injuries from flailing skis or from falls onto your own skis; they are also the best way of stopping a released ski from hurtling down the slope.

Today, ski brakes have gained universal accept-

Released ski brakes with arms pointing backward (**A**), and forward (**B**).

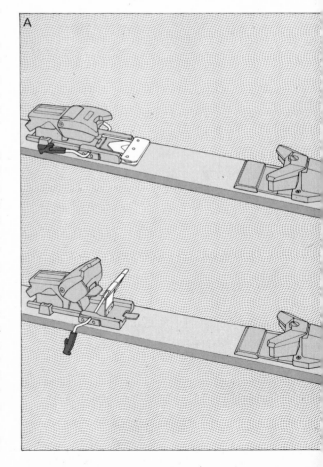

ance, and every manufacturer of bindings offers one or more models, most of which are integrated with bindings. Ski brakes, like bindings, are mechanical devices which require careful mounting, adjustment, and maintenance. If you intend to have brakes mounted on your skis, you should have a professional ski-shop mechanic do the job. The installation of a ski brake may affect the clearance between boot sole and binding and will probably require a readjustment of the binding.

Most ski brakes have two arms, both pointing either backward or forward when the brakes are in the cocked position and the boot is in the binding. The advantage of backward-pointing arms is that there is less risk of getting them hooked onto twigs

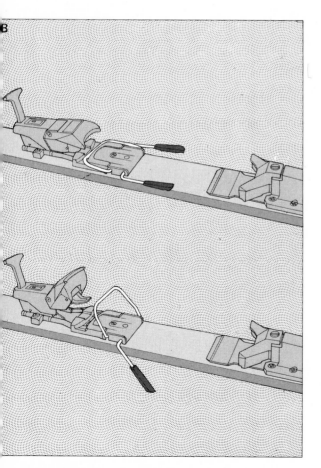

when you are skiing through brushwood. On some types of brake, the arms are tucked away so that they constitute a minimum overhang and do not increase the gliding resistance too much in deep snow.

On a well-designed ski brake, it should be possible to lock the brake arms in a position where they are out of the way when the ski's edges are to be re-sharpened or its base is to be waxed. Instead of having arms which can be locked in this manner, some brakes are constructed in such a way that they can easily be removed.

Ski Poles

As compared to skis, bindings, and boots, a ski pole is a relatively simple piece of equipment. It consists of grip, strap, shaft, basket, and tip. Although its construction is simple, a properly selected ski pole contributes considerably to skiing performance and safety.

The ski pole's contribution to the skier's performance depends on the proper planting of the pole. When watching a slalom racer, you will notice how intensely he uses his poles at each turn. The ease with which he plants them is due to the fact that he uses extremely light-weight, high-strength poles of a length carefully selected to match his skiing style.

A ski pole used for high-performance skiing must fulfil the following requirements:

1 Light weight (low swing-weight). The center of mass should be situated as closely as possible to the grip. For this reason, modern ski poles are tapered and have their smallest diameter near the basket. The shaft is either made of aircraft aluminum alloy, high-grade steel, or filament-wound fiberglass.

2 Tightly-fitting grip. A controlled pole-plant maneuver requires a perfect fit between the skier's hand and the grip.

Two basic types of grip are on the market today: the "classic" grip with a wrist strap, and the strapless grip. The strap serves two purposes: the first is that it permits the skier to retain his poles when he falls, and the second is that it allows for a tight joint between hand and pole during pushing actions. Since it runs round the wrist, thus increasing the area of support, the strap allows the skier a more powerful thrust with the pole. While standard straps are still widely used on low-price poles, breakaway straps are often used on expensive poles. Straps of the latter type come apart from the grip when they are subjected to a certain amount of load.

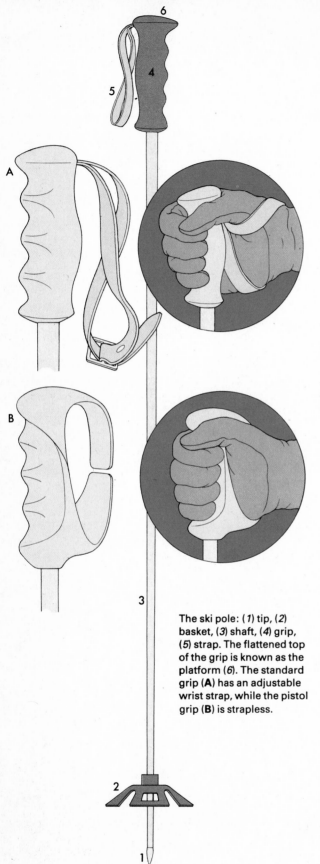

Modern poles have molded plastic grips, which are shaped to fit the anatomy of the hand perfectly. The strapless type of pole is getting an increasing market share, since it offers several advantages over poles with wrist straps. As a matter of fact, even strapless grips have a sort of strap; it mainly resembles fingers which buckle over the back of the hand. At the base of a strapless grip there is a platform on which the skier can rest his hand during pushing actions.

A ski pole of proper length will allow you to ski in a comfortable, balanced position. A pole which is too short forces the skier to bend over too much, while a pole which is too long forces him to maintain a too upright position. The rule of thumb for pole length selection has been changed several times, reflecting changes in skiing technique. Today, the following pole lengths are recommended:

Body height	Pole length
160 cm (63 inches)	up to 110 cm (43 inches)
165 cm (65 inches)	110–115 cm (43–45 inches)
170 cm (67 inches)	115–120 cm (45–47 inches)
175 cm (69 inches)	120–125 cm (47–49 inches)
180 cm (71 inches)	125–130 cm (49–51 inches)
185 cm (73 inches)	130–135 cm (51–53 inches)
190 cm (75 inches)	135–140 cm (53–55 inches)

Safety-Related Requirements of Ski Poles

Because of its functional design, the pole is a relatively dangerous part of the ski equipment. In order to minimize the risk of injury, safety standards which make certain features mandatory have been set up. In some countries (Germany, for instance), it is illegal to sell ski poles which do not meet the requirements of the safety standards. The most important of these requirements are:

1 The tip must not have a single point. Rounded or crown-like tips are mandatory, since these types of design allow for easy release from heavy snow and cannot inflict stab wounds.

2 The strap must either be separated from the grip or release the skier's hand if the pole should get caught in something. The basket must be designed in such a way that the chance of its getting caught is as small as possible.

3 The platform at the top of the grip must have a diameter larger than that of a human eye socket; further, it should be large enough to prevent impact injuries.

4 In case the skier falls onto the pole, its shaft must bend but not break, since splinters otherwise might cause injuries.

The ski pole: (1) tip, (2) basket, (3) shaft, (4) grip, (5) strap. The flattened top of the grip is known as the platform (6). The standard grip (**A**) has an adjustable wrist strap, while the pistol grip (**B**) is strapless.

3

THE BASICS

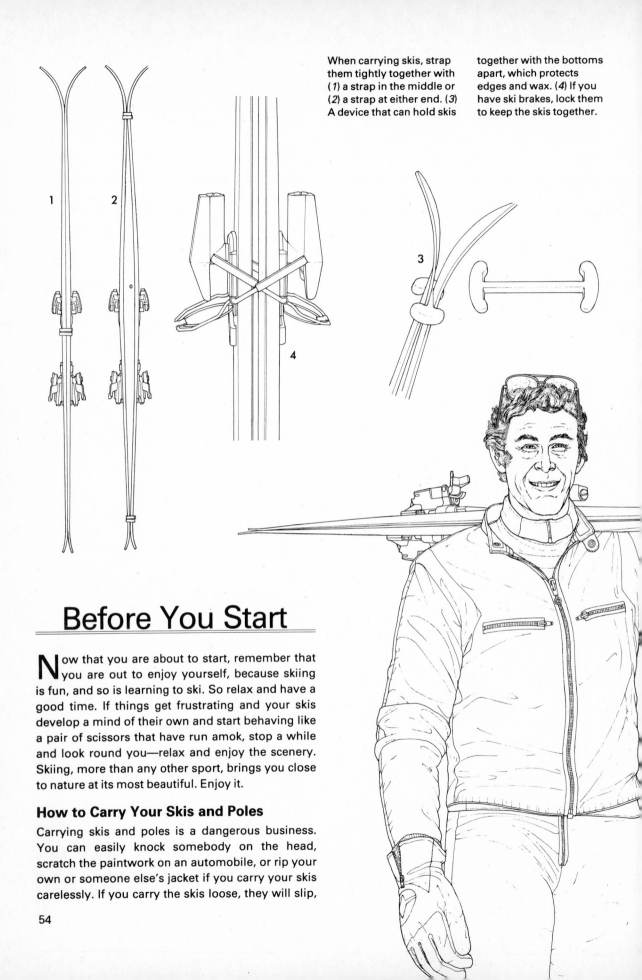

When carrying skis, strap them tightly together with (*1*) a strap in the middle or (*2*) a strap at either end. (*3*) A device that can hold skis together with the bottoms apart, which protects edges and wax. (*4*) If you have ski brakes, lock them to keep the skis together.

Before You Start

Now that you are about to start, remember that you are out to enjoy yourself, because skiing is fun, and so is learning to ski. So relax and have a good time. If things get frustrating and your skis develop a mind of their own and start behaving like a pair of scissors that have run amok, stop a while and look round you—relax and enjoy the scenery. Skiing, more than any other sport, brings you close to nature at its most beautiful. Enjoy it.

How to Carry Your Skis and Poles

Carrying skis and poles is a dangerous business. You can easily knock somebody on the head, scratch the paintwork on an automobile, or rip your own or someone else's jacket if you carry your skis carelessly. If you carry the skis loose, they will slip, ending up unbalanced and crossed, and this will cause a lot of irritation. Always strap the skis together, running surfaces face to face, with a strap or with one of the special ski-holding devices that are now on the market. If you have ski brakes, you can use them to lock the skis together.

When the skis are tightly held together, swing them over your shoulder, with the tips pointing ahead. The skis should lie flat, with the toe-pieces just behind your shoulder. You only have to keep a

Another way to carry skis—"military" style.

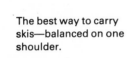

The best way to carry skis—balanced on one shoulder.

steadying hand in the forebody area in order to keep them balanced, and you can carry your poles in the same hand.

Another way to carry skis is to lean them against your shoulder and hold the tails in your hand, like a soldier carrying a rifle. You may have some trouble carrying them like this, since they will be unevenly balanced on your shoulder.

You can also carry your skis under your arm, but this is not recommended, as it is far too easy to hit someone or something when you turn round.

How to Stand on Your Skis

When putting on your skis, lay them first on the ground, with the right and left skis in their correct position. Don't throw your skis down; they are your skiing tools, so put them down carefully and you will keep them longer. Tiny arrows or marks on the toe- or heel-pieces indicate which is your right

and which is your left ski. Many people don't care about making sure that the correct ski is on the correct foot, but this is important, especially if you are interested in skiing well. The reason is that although most skis have the same sidecut on the inside as well as the outside of the ski, the bindings are adjusted to suit the left or the right foot. The steel edge on the inside wears out quicker than that on the outside, so that, after a time, the skis may be exchanged. Be sure, however, to adjust the bindings accordingly, when you switch skis.

Beginners usually cannot coordinate their movements very well and have difficulty in stepping into the bindings properly. Balance yourself with your ski poles and fit your toe into the toe-piece. To ensure a perfect fit, the boot sole must be free of snow and grit. If you have a step-in binding, step down on the heel-piece. The binding will lock and the boot will be held tightly to the ski.

If you have never stood on skis before, it is quite a tall order to be told to do so!

Of the three stances that skiers normally take, the wide stance gives the beginner the best lateral stability and good, all-round balance. In this stance the skis are kept 20–30 cm (8–12 inches) apart. The beginner should use it in the preliminary stages, such as "walking," straight running, and wedging. The drawback with this stance is that, if you want to transfer your weight from one ski's edge to the other, you must move your center of gravity sideways quite a bit, and this results in an increased response time (the time it takes for the skis to follow your orders).

As soon as you have familiarized yourself with your equipment and have gained some confidence, you should aim at the open, or natural, stance. This enables you to change edges more quickly, and you will find it easier to swivel your legs in a braquage (a foot, or steering, swivel). The skis should be 10–15 cm (4–6 inches) apart in this

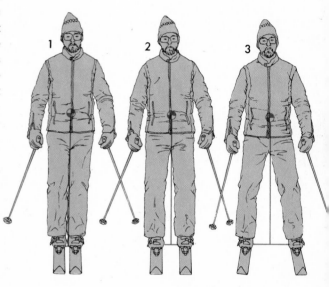

A To put on your skis. (1) Place them on the ground in the right order. (2) Support yourself on your poles while cleaning a boot sole. (3) Step into the binding, toe first. (4) Step down on the heel piece. (5, 6) Lock the heel piece by pulling up the release trigger. (7, 8) Putting on the other ski.
B The skiing stances: (1) narrow, (2) open, (3) wide.
C The natural position. Your center of gravity will be vertically over a point midway between your boots.

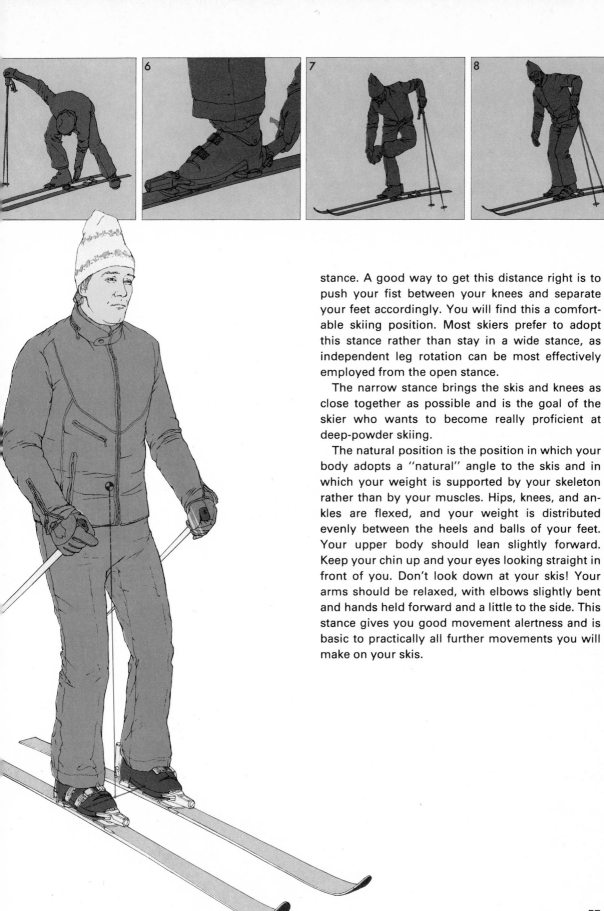

stance. A good way to get this distance right is to push your fist between your knees and separate your feet accordingly. You will find this a comfortable skiing position. Most skiers prefer to adopt this stance rather than stay in a wide stance, as independent leg rotation can be most effectively employed from the open stance.

The narrow stance brings the skis and knees as close together as possible and is the goal of the skier who wants to become really proficient at deep-powder skiing.

The natural position is the position in which your body adopts a "natural" angle to the skis and in which your weight is supported by your skeleton rather than by your muscles. Hips, knees, and ankles are flexed, and your weight is distributed evenly between the heels and balls of your feet. Your upper body should lean slightly forward. Keep your chin up and your eyes looking straight in front of you. Don't look down at your skis! Your arms should be relaxed, with elbows slightly bent and hands held forward and a little to the side. This stance gives you good movement alertness and is basic to practically all further movements you will make on your skis.

57

Your First Movements on Skis

For your first exercises on skis you should pick flat terrain with well-prepared snow. This is safest, because you cannot move without instigating the movement yourself and there is not very far to fall. Put your skis on, take your poles in your hands, and get ready. The following exercises will acquaint you with the feel of your skis.

1 Lift one ski at a time, keeping the ski tip on the ground. This will get you used to shifting your weight from one ski to the other.

2 To get yourself used to the weight of your skis, stand with both skis equally weighted. Then transfer your entire weight to one foot and lift the unweighted ski clear of the snow. Now swing the unweighted ski sideways over the weighted ski and back again. Crouch forward and repeat. Lean backward and repeat. Use your poles to support you.

3 Now start to "walk" on your skis without raising them from the ground. Put your weight on the left ski and slide the right ski forward. Now transfer your weight to the right ski and slide the left ski forward. Resist the temptation to let the ski tips lift from the ground. Keep your knees bent and take short, comfortable strides. Do this in a straight line at first and then start going in a circle. Slowly but surely you will start to get the hang of things and will begin to use the poles to glide a little as well. "Walking" with or without poles helps to develop your natural rhythm and balance. The other recommended exercises illustrated here develop balance also, and some of them will help you to learn a few of the basic maneuvers, such as turning while standing, and stepping uphill.

Sooner or later—probably sooner—you are going to have a fall. Don't worry about it; even the best skiers take some good ones now and then. Falling is a part of learning. If you feel yourself getting out of control or going off balance, don't fight it—fall. Crouch and bring your rear end to the ground first; then fall sideways. Try not to fall forward or backward. A sideways fall is usually harmless and will bring you to a skidding stop.

The best way to get up is to turn so that your skis are downhill (below you on the slope) and pointing across the hill (perpendicular to the fall line). Crouch so that your rear end is close to the skis, and bring your body over your boots. You can then get up by helping yourself with your hands or ski poles. Another way to get up is to plant a pole into the snow on the uphill side near your hips. Put your uphill hand on the basket and grab the top of the pole with your other hand. By pushing at the basket and pulling at the top you will soon be up.

Climbing Uphill

Another very important basic is how to sidestep up a hill. Now that you've learned to "walk" with your skis, find a nice, gentle slope for your first downhill runs. It should run out to a plateau at the end,

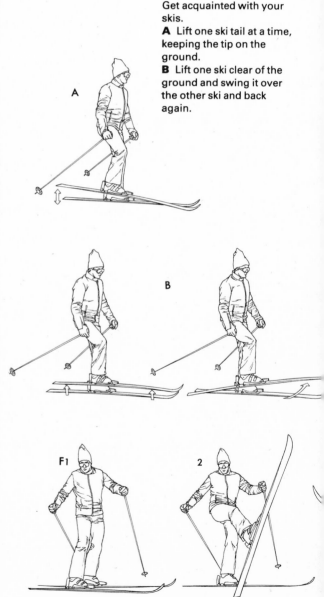

Get acquainted with your skis.
A Lift one ski tail at a time, keeping the tip on the ground.
B Lift one ski clear of the ground and swing it over the other ski and back again.

where you will come to a stop. It is even better if the plateau is short and ends in a slight uphill slope. But before you can make that first trip downhill, you must get to the top of the slope. The worst problem a beginner has in climbing a hill is that he glides two steps backward for every forward step he makes, and that can demoralize anyone. The thing to do is to keep your skis perpendicular to the fall line. With your knees bent and both knees and hips pushing sideways into the slope, you put your weight on the downhill ski, thus making its inside edge "bite" into the snow. Now lift your other ski uphill one step. Transfer your weight to the uphill ski and then lift up the downhill ski a step. Continue in this way until you are at the top. If you get your skis out of perpendicular, you may start to glide downhill, either forward or backward. Use your poles to support your sidestepping efforts and to stop fore and aft slipping. If you feel yourself slipping forward, bring your ski tips uphill a little; if

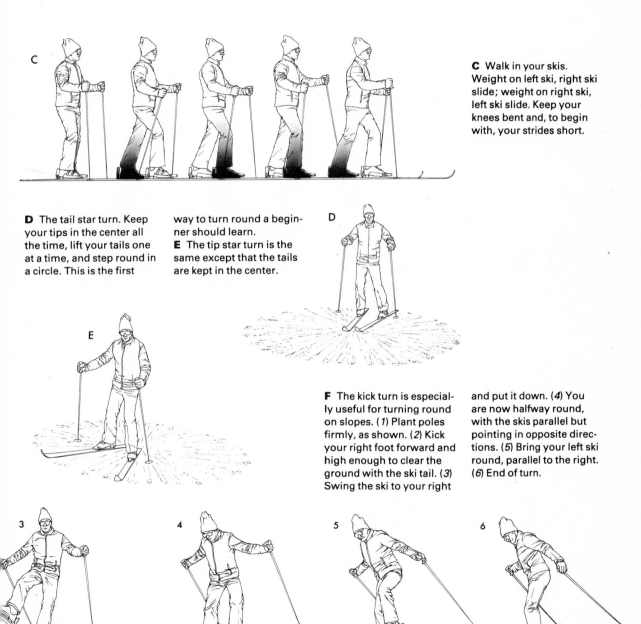

C Walk in your skis. Weight on left ski, right ski slide; weight on right ski, left ski slide. Keep your knees bent and, to begin with, your strides short.

D The tail star turn. Keep your tips in the center all the time, lift your tails one at a time, and step round in a circle. This is the first way to turn round a beginner should learn.
E The tip star turn is the same except that the tails are kept in the center.

F The kick turn is especially useful for turning round on slopes. (*1*) Plant poles firmly, as shown. (*2*) Kick your right foot forward and high enough to clear the ground with the ski tail. (*3*) Swing the ski to your right and put it down. (*4*) You are now halfway round, with the skis parallel but pointing in opposite directions. (*5*) Bring your left ski round, parallel to the right. (*6*) End of turn.

you feel yourself slipping backward, bring the tails uphill a little. Remember to take small steps and not to lift your feet too high. Another method of climbing uphill, known as "herringboning," is illustrated on this page (illustration **C**).

The First Downhill Run

You have now reached the summit of the slope and are ready for your first downhill run. Separate your skis by 20–25 cm (8–10 inches) and point them downhill. Your weight should be evenly distributed on your feet (the whole foot should feel weighted), and the skis should be flat, not edged. Relax into the natural position, hands in front, hips, knees, and ankles flexed forward, and the upper part of your body leaning slightly forward. Thrust firmly with the poles, and you are on your way. The exhilaration of your first downhill run will confirm for you that this is what it's all about—the joy of controlled motion on skis!

On subsequent downhill runs, try the following exercises, which will improve your balance.

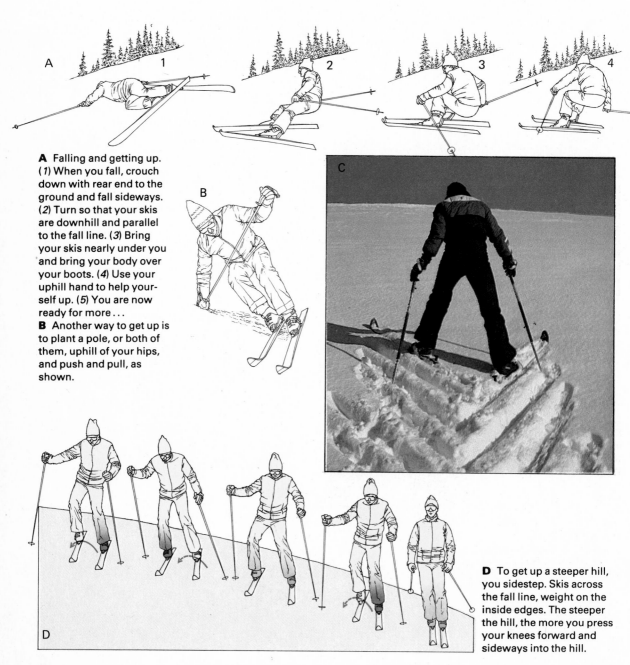

A Falling and getting up. (*1*) When you fall, crouch down with rear end to the ground and fall sideways. (*2*) Turn so that your skis are downhill and parallel to the fall line. (*3*) Bring your skis nearly under you and bring your body over your boots. (*4*) Use your uphill hand to help yourself up. (*5*) You are now ready for more...

B Another way to get up is to plant a pole, or both of them, uphill of your hips, and push and pull, as shown.

D To get up a steeper hill, you sidestep. Skis across the fall line, weight on the inside edges. The steeper the hill, the more you press your knees forward and sideways into the hill.

1 Bend several times and touch the toes of your boots.
2 Ski under a gate made of three slalom poles, two upright and one horizontal.
3 Lift the tail of the right and left ski alternately.
4 Step sideways out of and back into your track.
5 Place a glove or a pole on one side of the track and pick it up in passing, first with one hand and then with the other.

Practice these exercises with and without poles. It is better for your balance if you do them without.

So far, so good. When you are confident that you can do the above, it is time for the next stage, the uphill step turn. Before that, however, a word about what happens to you—and what you should do—on bumpy terrain.

Skiing Bumps and Hollows

There are bumps and hollows in every slope, no matter how smooth it looks. Hitting a bump can be quite a shock for the beginner—a bit like going over one of those old hump-backed bridges when

C The herringbone step, so called after the pattern it leaves in the snow, is used for climbing straight up a not-so-steep hill. Tails close together and tips out in a V; keep your weight on the inside edges of both skis. Left pole supports while right ski takes a step, and vice versa.

E Exercises to help you improve your balance and, thus, your confidence. While skiing downhill, you should (*1*) bend several times, flexing your knees, and touch the toes of your boots; (*2*) ski under a gate, as shown; (*3*) lift the tail of your right ski, put it down, then lift the tail of your left ski, put it down, and so on; (*4*) step sideways out of and back into your track; (*5*) pick up a glove or a pole in passing, first with one hand and then with the other.

driving. The thing to do is to use your knees as shock absorbers. Say that you are skiing downhill (in the natural position, as usual) and you reach a bump. Bend your knees and ankles sharply, pushing your hands forward to help you keep your balance. Then as you get to the top of the bump, let it push your knees even more into the bent position. As you go down the other side of the bump, straighten your legs and get back to the natural position immediately. In this way, you will absorb the bump without losing balance. Remember that

the shock is taken by the ankles and knees only. A bigger bump will, however, force you to bend at the hips, too.

Similarly, when you hit a "dip," straighten your legs somewhat and then flex your knees and ankles as you come up the other side of the dip.

The Uphill Step Turn

As you level out at the end of the easy slope, try the uphill step turn. Bend your legs somewhat and lift the tip of, say, your left ski slightly to the left. Plant

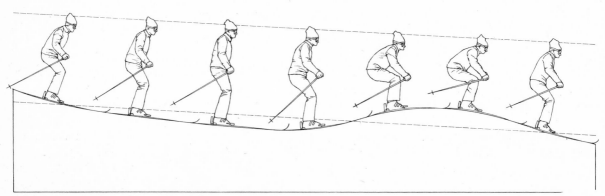

(ABOVE) Learning to ride the bumps is an important step in your skiing progress. Your knees function as shock absorbers to absorb the bumps in the terrain.

(BELOW) The uphill step turn is the first turn you learn for use while actually skiing. It is a series of tiny steps taken by lifting and moving slightly sideways one ski tip, and then the other, in the required direction.

it down and then lift the right ski tip and move the ski so that it is parallel to the left ski. Do this several times, using short steps, until you have turned the desired amount or until you stop. Practice the turn in the other direction, until you can turn with ease either to the left or to the right. This is the first and easiest way to change direction, to control speed, and to stop.

Using a Ski Lift

The first kind of aid skiers used to get to the top of a slope was bits of fur, which were applied to the ski bases with the furry side down and the hair growth angled to oppose the incline of the slope. This made it possible to ski up even steep slopes without sliding backwards. Today, skiers can travel from the bottom to the top of a slope with a minimum of effort by means of rope tows, T-bars, and chair-lifts. These types of lift are quite common in Europe, whereas T-bars nowadays are disappearing in the United States, where safety factors make them an insurance problem.

The Rope Tow

Rope tows are usually installed on gentle slopes used by beginners. When about to use a rope tow, slip the straps of your poles over the wrist of your outside hand (the one away from the rope) and sidestep to the rope, keeping your ski tips pointing directly uphill. The side from which you approach the rope will determine which hand you use first to grasp it. Always use your inside hand (the one nearest the rope), allowing the rope to slip gently through your gloved fingers. As you tighten your grip, you will slowly begin to move with the rope as it tows you uphill. Keep your arms straight and your skis equally weighted and in the tracks. Your knees should be flexible and bent to absorb any uneven terrain. To slow down because of any problems ahead of you, relax your grip on the rope and let it slide through your fingers (as you did when you started, to avoid a sudden jerk), but don't let it go.

As you near the top of the slope, prepare to release your grip and step quickly out of the track, to make room for the skier behind you. Newer models of the rope tow have fixed handles that are easier to grip. Most rope tows operate without attendants, so be careful and study the procedure before you start.

The T-bar or J-bar

Another type of lift is the T-bar or J-bar, which consists of a series of T- or J-shaped bars attached to a moving cable. T-bars normally accommodate two people, J-bars, one person only.

The lift operator will pull the bar down and forward to a position under your buttocks, at the back of your thighs. Don't sit down. Stay standing and keep your skis parallel, equally weighted, and pointing uphill. Hold on with your inside hand and let the bar pull you uphill. Keep your knees bent to absorb the terrain and watch the tracks carefully.

Sometimes, you will find tracks with double fall lines or with one track higher than the other. You can adjust to this quite easily by letting one ski ride slightly behind the other. When riding without a partner, never put the T-bar between your legs. This could be dangerous. When two arrive at an unloading station together, the more experienced partner should allow the other to ski off the track by tilting the bar. He should then twist the cross bar to the vertical position and release it gently, so that it does not swing and become snarled at the lift towers or with the main cable. *Never* embark or disembark in the middle of the slope.

(*LEFT*) To use a rope tow. (*1*) Slip your pole straps over your outside wrist. (*2*) Let the rope slip through your fingers. (*3*) Tighten your grip, keeping your arms straight, and the rope will tow you along. (*4*) At the unloading station, let the rope go with your outside hand and step away with your outside ski. (*5*) Let go with your inside hand and step away with your inside ski. (*6*) Move away from the rope tow. (*RIGHT*) To use the Poma lift. (*1–3*) Back your ski tails against the stop board. When you get the disk from the operator, place it between your legs, as shown. (*4*) Keep your skis parallel and your knees flexed. (*5*) When disembarking, hold the bar with

Poma Lifts

The Poma lift consists of poles hung on a cable; each pole has a disk-like plate attached to its base.

The operator will pull the disk down when you are ready and either give it to you or place it between your legs so that it presses squarely in the back of your thighs below your buttocks. Your position should be the same as in the rope-tow, with your arms straight, knees slightly bent, and general body position relaxed. The pole of a Poma lift is spring-loaded, just like the rope of the J- or T-bar, so you will start off with a slight jerk. When you are under way and feel comfortable, the bar can be held with one hand only. Keep your skis parallel and knees flexed to absorb the terrain. Hold on to the bar with both hands as you arrive at

To use the T-bar. (*1*) Back your ski tails up against the stop board; watch the approaching bar over your inside shoulder. (*2*) The lift operator pulls the bar down to the back of your thighs. Don't sit down! (*3*) Hold the rope with your inside hand and your poles

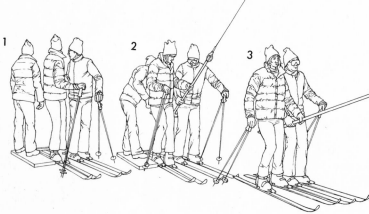

both hands, bend your legs, and disengage the disk. (*6*) Move away quickly.

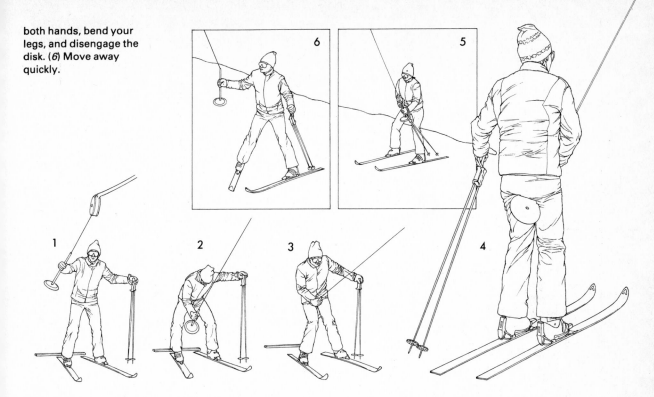

the unloading station, then bend your legs and disengage the Poma disk. Embark or disembark *only* at designated stations. It is dangerous for yourself and other skiers to do otherwise.

Chair-lifts

The chair-lift is the most common and most preferred system of transportation for longer, steeper slopes. There are single, double, triple, and even quadruple chair-lifts. The chair-like device is suspended from a cable by a single or double bar. The most common is the double chair-lift. Chair-lifts do not require the skier's contact with the terrain. When boarding a double chair, both passengers should step quickly into the position indicated by markers or by the lift attendant. If you are wearing your skis, carry your poles in your inside hand. Each of you should watch carefully for the oncoming chair over your outside shoulder and, as it approaches, grasp the bar with your outside hand and sit down gently. Immediately close the safety-bar and place your skis on the lower rest-bar. If you embark holding your skis, keep poles and skis with your outside. (*4*) The bar *pulls*, not pushes, you up the slope. (*5*) At the unloading station, the more experienced skier tilts the bar so that the other can step away from the bar. (*6*) He then twists the bar to vertical to let himself off. (*7*) He releases the bar gently.

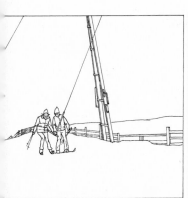

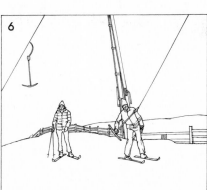

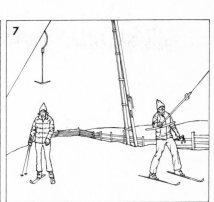

Although this double chair-lift has a safety bar, it has no rest-bar for the skis. Care must be taken at points where the terrain is close, so that ski tips do not get stuck in the snow.

under your outside arm, and be careful that no one gets hurt when you are dismounting at the lift station. When boarding a single chair-lift, step quickly into the indicated position, as above. Sometimes, hooks are provided for your poles. Use them. Don't swing your feet, as this will swing the whole cable and other chairs too. When approaching points where the terrain is close, hold your skis well up to prevent catching a tip in the snow. Approaching the unloading station, open the safety bar, hold your poles in your outside hand and keep your ski tips up until clear of the ramp. If the unloading station is on level ground, stand up at the marked point and ski off quickly to clear the ramp for the next skier. If the station is on an incline, ski down the ramp, turning to the opposite of your partner to avoid collision. Duck to avoid the overhead chairs as you ski away. Be very sure not to hook any part of your clothing or equipment on the chair. *Double-check for this as you approach the unloading station.* Always read all instructions posted at the stations and along the route of the lift.

If you fall while using a T-bar, immediately let go. Don't allow yourself to be dragged along. Listen always to the lift operators' advice. That's why they are there.

Other Transportation

Cable cars and gondolas provide mass transportation and are quite easy to use. Remember that you must take your skis off. Stand or sit inside the cable cars. The small gondola cabins seat three or four people, and loading and unloading takes place inside the stations.

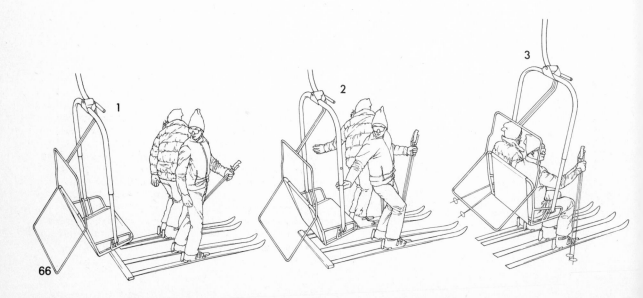

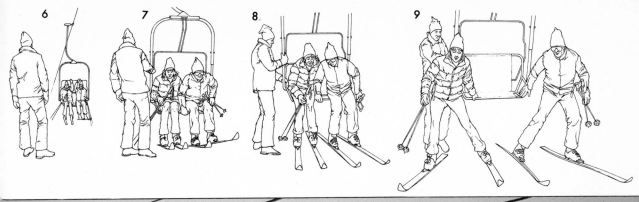

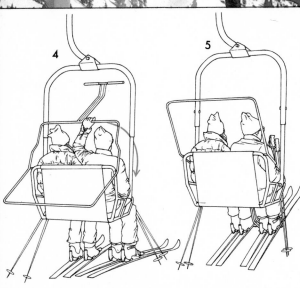

To use a double chair-lift. (*1*) Get your ski tails up against the stop boards and watch the approaching lift over your outside shoulder. (*2*) Grasp the bar with your outside hand. (*3*) Sit down gently and transfer your poles to your outside hand. (*4*) Pull down the safety bar. (*5*) Rest your skis on the rest-bar. (*6*) As you approach disembarkation, lift up the safety bar. (*7*) Prepare to get up. Check that no part of your clothing or equipment is hooked on the chair. (*8*) The attendant holds the lift as you get up. (*9*) Ski away from the lift. (*ABOVE*) A triple chair-lift.

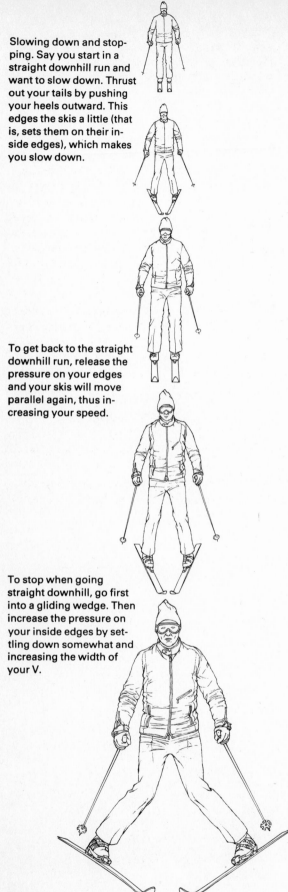

Slowing down and stopping. Say you start in a straight downhill run and want to slow down. Thrust out your tails by pushing your heels outward. This edges the skis a little (that is, sets them on their inside edges), which makes you slow down.

To get back to the straight downhill run, release the pressure on your edges and your skis will move parallel again, thus increasing your speed.

To stop when going straight downhill, go first into a gliding wedge. Then increase the pressure on your inside edges by settling down somewhat and increasing the width of your V.

Further Basic Maneuvers

You can now ski straight downhill, surviving the bumps and hollows that are "hidden" in the most innocent-looking slope, and you can use the uphill step turn to change direction and even stop. Also, you know how to use the various types of ski lifts (although you will not go to the steep slopes yet). The following maneuvers will form your basic skiing skills, on which you will base all your further prowess.

The Gliding Wedge

The gliding wedge is an important way to control speed and a good method of getting your skis into the best starting position for a change of direction. To make a wedge, simply push your ski tails apart, so that the skis are in a V-position that is not quite closed at the top. You can do this from a stationary natural position by pushing the tails outward, or by stepping or jumping into the V-position. Then, with some help from your poles, start downhill. Keep your skis as flat as possible and weighted as for a straight run downhill. (The effect this will have will be to set the skis slightly on their inside edges.) The tracks you make in the snow should show two parallel lines that have been made by the tails of your skis (with, naturally, variations for any unevenness or bumps on the slope). When you have practiced this a few times, you can combine a straight run and a gliding wedge.

Straight Run—Gliding Wedge—Straight Run

Start downhill in a straight run, then gradually turn your heels outward so that the skis form a wedge. Keep the wedge narrow and comfortable. To get back to the straight run, release the pressure on the inside edges, and the skis will move back parallel to each other again. Keep your hands waist-high and in front of you to the sides.

This combination of the straight run and the gliding wedge will get you acquainted with the feel of your ski edges. Another way to get this feel while going straight downhill is to bend your knees and push them to one side so that your ski edges bite into the snow. Now "roll" your knees over to the other side, and your skis will change edges.

From a Gliding to a Braking Wedge

When you start to pick up speed in a gliding wedge, you can slow down with a braking wedge.

The wedge turn is a continuation of the gliding wedge. The secret of the wedge turn is that the turn follows the track of the weighted ski. From a straight run downhill, go into a gliding wedge (if you want to start slowly, begin with a gliding wedge). Now put a little more weight or pressure on one ski (here, the right) and edge it slightly. You will start to turn to your left.

This is done by increasing the pressure on the inside edges of your skis by settling down, that is, by crouching with your center of gravity over your boots.

The Wedge Turn

You have already learned the first way of changing direction, the uphill step turn, and now that you have mastered the technique of controlling speed by putting pressure on your inside edges, you are ready to try the wedge turn, which is the most basic way to change direction by using your edges.

Starting from a gliding wedge, you begin a wedge turn by putting a little more weight or pressure (which has been evenly distributed over the skis) onto one of the skis, at the same time edging it slightly on its inside edge. You will then begin to turn. If you put more weight on the left ski, you will turn to the right; if on the right ski, to the left. (The weighted ski will turn in the direction in which it is turned in the wedge.) The ski on which you put more weight is usually known as the outside ski, as it ends up on the outside of the turn.

Different Exercises and Games to Improve Balance

1 Make turns round slalom poles or similar markings while on a flat piece of ground.
2 Following a circular path on a slope, climb to the top of the slope, turn, ski down, step out of track, and climb again.

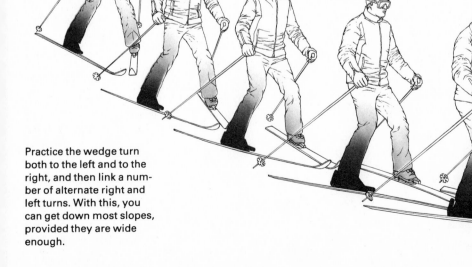

Practice the wedge turn both to the left and to the right, and then link a number of alternate right and left turns. With this, you can get down most slopes, provided they are wide enough.

3 Get two others to ski down a slope with you, holding hands, and bend and stretch together.

4 Set up a parallel slalom course with ten to fifteen gates, and match your newly learned skills with those of other beginners, using the gliding wedge and wedge turn. The course should be set along the fall line. Establish your rhythm as soon as possible after the start.

5 Another game which is both fun and good for your sense of balance is played by two teams. Set up two equal courses with single poles down the fall line. Each skis down to the first pole, brakes, steps round the pole, continues down to the next pole, and so on, until the finish. Then the next member of the team follows suit, and the first team to finish wins.

6 Two skiers form a team and try to catch a third skier while he is skiing down a slope. You may only touch the pursued skier with your hand when you catch him. The man to be chased starts on the slope above the two-man team. This game requires quick reflexes and the ability to make quick stops. Choose a gentle slope, so that your speed won't become too high.

(*RIGHT*) One of the main problems you encounter when learning the traverse is sideslipping, that is, gliding sideways down the hill when your skis have lost their grip on the snow. The secret is to edge your skis so that the uphill edges bite into the snow. The steeper the slope, the greater the edge bite should be. (*1*) On a gentle slope. (*2*) On a moderately steep slope. (*3*) On a steep slope.

The Traverse

Traversing means skiing diagonally across a hill instead of going down the fall line. The natural position is again used: open-stance ankles, knees flexed, and the upper body bent slightly forward for balance. Your uphill ski must be slightly ahead of the downhill ski, which will hold more of your weight. This means that your downhill knee will be slightly behind the uphill knee. Both knees should be slightly bent, but not too much, because you will need some bending reserve to control your turning and to absorb shocks from bumps in the terrain. The uphill edges of both skis should bite into the snow to prevent you from slipping sideways down the hill. The softer the snow, the less knee angulation you will need to hold the edges (that is, to keep them biting). Knee angulation is pressing the bent knees sideways into the hill so that the edges of the skis bite into the snow. It is all that is necessary to hold the edges on a shallow slope, but on steeper slopes with hard-packed snow, you must also use hip angulation. It is important that your downhill ski has the same edge set (that is, that its base makes the same angle against the slope) as the uphill ski, so you must press your downhill knee more firmly into the hill. The more you bend your knees forward, the more you can angulate them by driving them into the hill. People with reduced mobility in the hips will always have problems with the traverse, because

The traverse is a major item in every skier's repertoire. It consists of skiing across a hill rather than straight downhill. The steeper the line of the traverse, the faster you go.

even the sharpest edges are worthless without angulation. The way to control your traverse is to stay nearly square on your skis and move your knees and hips into the hill, while facing your upper body toward the valley, bending slightly from the waist. Keep your hands forward and to the side, holding your poles tightly—be careful not to drag the poles behind you.

To practice the traverse you should find a wide, open slope that allows a long running distance. Ski across the slope in both directions, not only in the one you find most comfortable. In fact, it is a general rule that you should *always* practice skiing movements in both directions—left and right—as you are not going to spend your skiing career making only left-hand or right-hand turns!

You will need lots of practice before you can perform a perfectly edged traverse without skidding, but the traverse is fun, so you will not find practice boring. Start by trying to traverse in the open stance; it will give you better balance and allow you more room to move your knees into the hill, thus bringing the skis on edge. When you get used to moving your edges into the hill, you will be able to adopt a more narrow stance. If you feel your downhill ski sliding away, press your knees and your hips further into the hill. To hold your balance you will have to tip your upper body sideways and outward "into the valley." This is a real problem for most beginners, as it seems more natural—and safer, too!—to lean in toward the hill. This puts all the weight on the uphill ski and usually results in a fall into the hill. To avoid this, keep your knees and, if necessary, hips bent into the hill, while your upper body turns slightly the other way. This bend of the body is known by the French as angulation and by Americans as the comma position.

Two exercises will help you to stop your upper body from leaning into the hill when traversing.

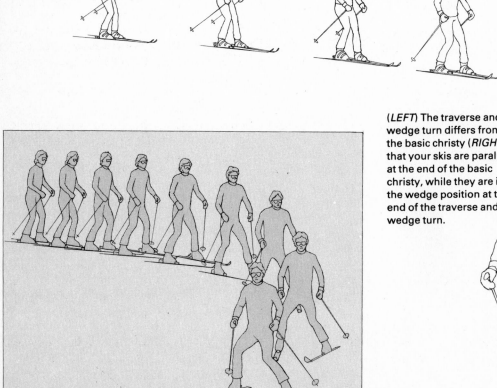

(*LEFT*) The traverse and wedge turn differs from the basic christy (*RIGHT*) in that your skis are parallel at the end of the basic christy, while they are in the wedge position at the end of the traverse and wedge turn.

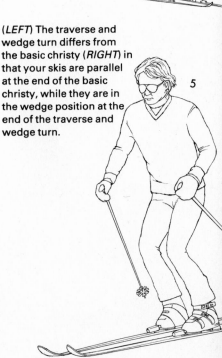

1 Balance on your downhill ski while lifting your uphill ski's tail off the snow.

2 Reach down with your downhill hand and touch the calf of your downhill leg.

At the end of your traverse, you can stop by a simple uphill step turn, but a better and more elegant way to end the traverse is with an uphill christy (see pp. 78–79).

The traverse is a very important part of the skier's repertoire and is used to begin many skiing movements.

The Traverse and the Wedge Turn

You have now learned how to master the wedge turn and the traverse. The next step is to combine them. Begin by traversing the hill in a relaxed natural position, with most of your weight carried on your downhill ski, and your knees, ankles, and upper body bent slightly forward. Push one or both skis into a wedge (it makes no difference which ski

The main movements of the basic christy. Each number refers to the corresponding number mentioned in the main text (*see RIGHT*).

you push out to form the wedge, if you choose not to use both skis). When the skis are in the wedge position, your weight should be equally distributed on both skis until you reach the fall line. Now shift your weight more to the outside ski, so that you will continue to turn. When the turn is finished, let the skis gradually move back into the parallel open stance and start to traverse in the opposite direction. The more weighted, outside ski of the wedge turn will then become your downhill ski.

The Basic Christy

Now that you have learned (and, hopefully, become accomplished at) the traverse and the wedge turn, you are ready to try your hand at the first of the christies, the basic christy. (Christy comes from the old name for Oslo, Christiania, where this turn was developed.) As the sideslip, which is the distinguishing part of the turn, requires higher speeds than the wedge turn, you should go to a steeper slope. The stages of the basic christy are the following.

1 Begin with a rather steep traverse in the open stance.

2 Go into a gliding wedge.

3 Increase the pressure on the inner edge of your outside ski. Your turn now commences.

4 Move your inside knee toward the center of the turn; match your inside ski (that is, bring it parallel to the outside ski), thus changing its edge set from the inside to the outside.

5 With your skis now parallel and slightly edge-set, you begin to sideslip.

6 To stop the sideslip, set your edges somewhat harder (it will stop by itself when you get into more of a traverse); you will continue in a new traverse, now in the opposite direction. Continue until you have accomplished a whole series of basic christies.

Unweighting

Unweighting is a momentary lightening of the skier's and skis' combined weight on the snow, which makes it easier for him to turn both feet simultaneously in a new direction. It is accomplished by up-unweighting (also called lift) or down-unweighting (leg retraction).

Unweighting is often described as a down–up–down movement. The first down movement is merely the reflexive preparation to the up movement and is accomplished by a crouching motion that results in a lowering of the center of gravity and a flexing of the knees. During the up movement, the body does not become fully erect, as the knees must stay somewhat flexed. It is during this movement that skier's and skis' weight on the snow lessens and the skis are pivoted in a new direction. In the final down movement, the rotation has begun and the turn's radius is determined by the speed of the down movement and the amount of steering and edging. The faster the down movement, the shorter the radius of the turn.

In the basic christy, up-unweighting can be a help when you set your edges harder to stop your sideslip. However, its real importance in the basic christy lies in that it gives the turn its proper rhythm.

Down-unweighting is a faster movement than up-unweighting and requires quicker reflexes. To do this, you suddenly draw your feet up while sharply flexing your knees. The advantage is that you are immediately ready to pivot your skis in the desired direction without having to sink first, as in up-unweighting. Down-unweighting is used in shorter, quicker turns on uneven terrain (christies on moguls or in deep powder). These are more advanced maneuvers and should not be tried until you have left the beginner stage and become an accomplished skier.

Up-unweighting in the basic christy. (*1*) Traverse in the open, natural stance. (*2*) Preparatory to unweighting, sink down. (*3*) Lift yourself up and pivot your skis. (*4*) Sink down, setting your edges. (*5*) Back to the open, natural stance.

Down-unweighting (*IN-SET*) is a more advanced movement. Flex your knees sharply, drawing your feet up quickly, thus unweighting the skis and allowing you to pivot quickly.

4

THE ABLE SKIER

The natural stop is the stop which children seem to be able to do naturally. Adults find it more difficult to learn, but it is most valuable and leads to other maneuvers, such as sideslipping. When you are heading downhill in the natural position and want to stop, you must pivot your skis hard across the fall line and flex your knees and ankles quickly and forcefully. Only your legs should pivot; keep your head and upper body pointing down the hill. The idea of the dropping movement is to put a lot of pressure on your heels, so that the skis go into a skidding stop.

When stopping on a slope in this way, always stop below another skier standing on the slope, not directly above him, for even if you are an expert, there is always the danger of misjudgment, resulting in an accident.

The Sideslip

With the sideslip you can check (slow down), put the finishing touches to a turn, pass safely through tricky terrain, or lose height with control and comfort if the slope is too steep for turning.

When your skis are perpendicular to the fall line on a steep hill and you have them flat, they will begin to slide sideways straight down the fall line. When you edge them, they will bite into the snow, and this allows you to control the slide sideways. On a gentle slope, your skis will hardly slide at all if you set the edges too hard. Now consider what happens on steeper terrain. Place yourself in the natural position, with your skis across the fall line. Your uphill ski should lead, and your upper body should be turned slightly downhill. The more you bend your knees and ankles forward, the more you

A The natural stop. (*1*) Go downhill in the natural position. (*2*) Pivot your skis hard across the fall line. (*3*) Flex your knees and ankles quickly and forcefully, so that you skid to a stop. Remember to pivot your legs only; head and upper body should face downhill all the time.

B The sideslip. (*1*) Stand in a not-too-gentle slope in the natural position with your skis across the fall line. Let your uphill ski lead, and turn your upper body slightly downhill. Bend your knees and ankles forward and move your knees sideways into the hill to set the edges of your skis. (*2*) Now make an up-motion of your whole body and move your knees back over the skis. As your skis flatten against the snow, you will begin to sideslip. To stop the sideslip, slant your knees into the hill again.

C The three types of sideslip: (*1*) straight down the fall line, (*2*) diagonal backward—you achieve this by transferring your weight to your heels—and (*3*) diagonal forward, caused by your transferring your weight to the balls of your feet.

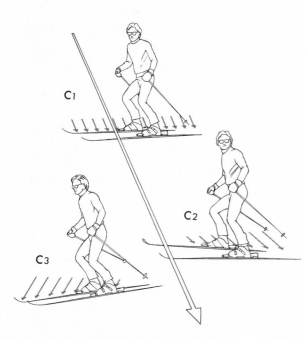

can move your knees sideways into the hill, thus setting the edges of your skis. At the same time, move your upper body sideways (into the valley) to maintain balance. Now move your knees back over the skis and, as your skis flatten against the snow, their edges will lose grip and you will begin to sideslip. By slanting your knees into the hill again, the edges of your skis will again catch, and you will check. With an up-motion of the whole body, you can again flatten your skis, making them lose their grip and start sliding again.

Remember that you control your sideslip by the amount of edging of your skis, suiting this to the snow conditions and the steepness of the slope.

There are three kinds of sideslip: the sideslip straight down the fall line, the diagonal forward sideslip, and the diagonal backward sideslip. All three are performed with open or closed skis in the parallel position and with the upper body in the position used for the traverse. Practice this on a fairly steep slope of well-packed but not icy snow.

When you have mastered the straight sideslip, try the diagonal sideslip. Shift your weight to the balls of your feet while straight sideslipping, and you will notice that you have begun to sideslip diagonally forward. Now transfer your weight to your heels, and you will find that you are changing to a diagonal backward sideslip. Actually, the diagonal sideslip is quite easy. Many people have difficulty in maintaining their edges in an ordinary traverse, especially when, with increasing speed, the forces acting on the edges increase and you need better-trained muscles and a more developed sense of balance and technique to keep the edges biting properly. The result is that poorly performed traverses end up as diagonal sideslips! As in the traverse, everybody will prefer to sideslip in one direction or the other, but you should practice sideslipping in both directions.

If you have trouble starting a sideslip, try a good push with both your poles uphill. If, at the same time, you do an up-motion, the grip of your ski edges will be released, and you will begin to sideslip. To control your speed as you sideslip, play with the edges of your skis by rolling your knees and ankles into and away from the hill; stay in the natural position. Remember that you will sideslip slower if you roll knees and ankles into the hill, and faster if you roll them away.

The Uphill Christy

This is a form of forward sideslip, a change of direction in which the skis are kept parallel. It is begun from a traverse and brings you uphill instead of down and over the fall line. The uphill christy is a very efficient way of controlling speed and is the final part of a great many turns. You can do it from various angles of traverse or even

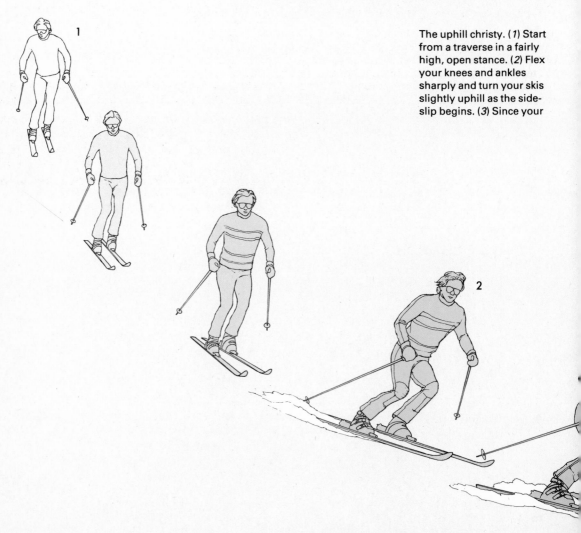

The uphill christy. (*1*) Start from a traverse in a fairly high, open stance. (*2*) Flex your knees and ankles sharply and turn your skis slightly uphill as the sideslip begins. (*3*) Since your

straight down the fall line, in which case it is called a christy off the fall line.

Starting from a traverse and in a rather high open stance, you lower your center of gravity by sharply flexing your knees and ankles. Simultaneously, you turn your skis slightly uphill as the sideslip begins. This causes the front edges to carve into the snow more than the tail edges and results in the skis' turning uphill. The more you edge and the more you weight the front part of your skis, the sharper the uphill turn will be. Keep your upper body facing in the direction of your original traverse. If you move your hips away from the hill or rotate them, you will turn too much uphill, so keep your upper body still, and remember that it is your knees and ankles that control the uphill christy, not your hips or upper body. Increase the steepness of your traverses until you are skiing the fall line and your uphill

front edges now carve more than your tail edges, you will start to turn uphill. (4) Steer into the turn with increased knee pressure. Keep your upper body facing downhill all through

the turn and don't rotate your hips or move them away from the hill. (5) Press your knees sideways into the slope during the turn, and ski the uphill christy to a stop.

christies are taking you out of it and then up to your left or right. To be able to ski a controlled uphill christy to a stop is an important step forward in your skiing technique. This turn needs good coordination, complete edge control, and a sure knowledge of when and how to shift your weight. It leads to the advanced christy and is the springboard to advanced skiing.

The Advanced, or Stem, Christy

The advanced christy begins like the basic christy, with a traverse, and it ends with an uphill christy and a traverse in the opposite direction. As you traverse, bring your uphill ski out into a V-position by pushing the ski tail out with your foot. In this position, ski to the fall line with your skis equally weighted. As you approach the fall line, shift more of your weight from the inside to the outside ski, which then will start to steer the turn. Release the inner edge on your less weighted, inside ski and match it with the outside ski. Then steer both skis into an uphill christy.

When you start the turn in the V-position, your outside ski will be on its inside edge already and will stay on it throughout the turn. You will find that, as you go faster when linking your advanced christies, your skis will tend to skid as in the uphill christy. In the fall line, your greatest difficulty will be to shift your weight from the turn's inside to its outside ski and to match the skis. Your speed will increase the less the edge-hold and the narrower

the V-position you have. High speed can give you balance problems and is best controlled with an uphill christy toward the end of the one turn just before you begin with the first part of the next turn.

As you practice the advanced christy, your confidence will grow, and it will become easier for you to judge how much you need to vary your speed as you approach the fall line, by pushing out your uphill ski. Remember that the wider your stem, the more you must bring your inside ski toward your outside ski when matching them. It is important that you master this technique if you are going to be skiing in steep terrain or if you are going to be negotiating bumps and moguls. It is also helpful to know this technique when you are learning how to make step turns.

At the start of an advanced christy, you will find it easier to stem out your uphill ski and to change its edge to form the V-position, if you use a pole plant. However, if you depend too much on your pole, you may take to leaning into the turn too much, thus losing your natural position and edge grip.

Using Your Ski Poles

Your ski poles are a very important part of your equipment. They are used not only for pushing forward on level terrain, but also for climbing.

Furthermore, they will give you confidence, particularly in the beginning, when you use them mainly for balance. Later, you will see how important they are also for rhythm and timing, when you are skiing short turns or on steep slopes. Pole work is an integral part of modern technique, and it is very important that you learn how to handle your poles properly.

In straight runs, wedge turns, and traverses, your

(*TOP*) The advanced christy. (*1*) Start out in a traverse and (*2*) push the tail of your uphill ski out with your foot. (*3*) With skis equally weighted, ski toward the fall line. (*4*) As you approach the fall line, weight your outside ski more so that you start to turn. (*5*) Release the inner edge of your inside ski and match it to your outside ski. (*6*) Steer your parallel skis into an uphill christy. (*ABOVE*) How to plant a pole. When initiating a turn, just as you start shifting your weight to your outside ski, turn the under edge of your downhill fist slightly upward and outward, as shown here. As the pole touches the snow, your hand moves forward and downward, and you use the planted pole as the pivot of your turn.

poles should be used primarily for balance, but in more advanced turns your pole can be used to initiate and to aid turning. Your wrists, not your arms, should be used in the pole plant; the position of your arms and hands should remain more or less the same throughout your skiing. If you move your entire arm to make a pole plant, your upper body will "follow" too much, and you may well lose your balance.

When planting a pole, turn the under edge of your fist slightly outward. Your hand and wrist move forward and you start to shift your weight to the outside ski. As the pole touches the snow, your hand and wrist move down, so that when your pole has been planted and you continue on your way, it should be in the same position that it had when you started the plant. Remember to let the plant come from your wrist; should it come from your arm and shoulder, there will be a tendency for the pole to lag behind, thus throwing you off balance. The planted pole is always the pivot of your turn.

In very advanced skiing, the ski pole is a somewhat secondary factor (because of the high speed involved, the skier has less time to make pole plants), but it is nonetheless important, since it helps the skier to establish the rhythm and timing necessary in quick turns, when skiing moguls, and on steep slopes.

Stemming and Stepping

Stemming and stepping are more closely related to the natural way of moving, that is, walking and running, than are parallel turns, which require both feet to be pivoted simultaneously. Stemming and stepping means moving the legs in a one–two sequence into your turn. It is a combination of independent leg action and rotation. Stemming one ski from the other causes the skis to spread apart. Some of the different maneuvers in which the skis are stemmed are the wedge, the down stem, the up stem, the parallel step, and racing steps.

Stemming and stepping are commonly used by beginners and intermediate skiers. Stemming is the easiest and most effortless way to start a turn, and it permits you to either stay with the turn or abandon it as you wish. The basic christy and the stem christy are stem turns.

The intermediate skier uses more deliberate stemming methods than the beginner to accomplish an edge change and weight shift. The size of the stem angle and its duration are determined by the skier's speed, the snow conditions, and the terrain.

The more advanced skier will use all kinds of stepping action, thus confirming his intimate relationship with speed, snow conditions, and terrain. The racer will use all of these stepping actions, too, when running a slalom or giant slalom course. He will use stepping to accelerate, to gain height toward the next gate, and to align with it. The down stem and the up stem have a one-leg, push-off motion but different turning movements.

The Up Stem

As you traverse, stem your uphill ski while holding the edge of the downhill ski. This will make your uphill ski point in the direction of your new turn. Now, smoothly start to transfer your weight to the inner edge of the outside ski of your turning arc, that is, to your former uphill ski. Match your inside ski to finish the turn in an uphill christy. Do this by

crouching and pivoting your skis in the new direction. Your next turn should start with an up-motion as you once again stem your uphill ski.

In the up stem, your ski will be turned and change edges while off the snow. A pole plant will help you to unweight your downhill ski and to match it. The up stem will help you to master the art of skiing on bumpy slopes, as it allows you to stem right at the top of the moguls.

When skiing on steep and icy terrain, you will find that the steering phase mentioned above is much more difficult. The less your ski tail moves out of your turning arc, the better you will be able to carve your turns. Try fast sliding and stopping in sequences on many different terrains and in varying snow conditions. You will gradually get the feel for correct balance by weight shifting and edge control.

The Down Stem

The down stem is a "one-leg check and rebound" movement in which you first push out your downhill ski to get a grip for its inside edge and to build a platform for the rebound. From a previous turn or traverse, push your downhill ski into a down stem. Your downhill leg is bent and your downhill knee is pushed into the hill, thus engaging the inside edge of your ski hard. A strong push-off from your downhill ski will transfer your weight to the other ski (that is, the turn's outside ski). Simultaneously, your outside leg starts to turn, you change edges, and you begin to steer. (To steer is to control the later part of a turn by edge setting, pressure control by weight transfer, and leg rotation.) By matching your inside ski after the stem, you can add substantially to your turning motion. Use steering leverage and leg rotation to control the rest of the turn.

To do an up stem, start by traversing in a fairly crouched position. (*1*) Do an up-motion to unweight your skis, and stem your uphill ski while holding the edge of your downhill ski. (*2*) Smoothly transfer your weight to the inner edge of your stemmed ski and (*3*) match your inside ski. Finish the turn in an uphill christy by crouching and pivoting your skis in the new direction.

Steering leverage is moving your center of gravity forward or backward along the skis; this helps to determine the radius of the turn. Varying intensities of the push-off from the down stem should be coordinated with the intended radius of the turn.

Note that, so far, balance has been achieved without pole plants. You can establish better rhythm by planting the pole at the same moment that your downhill ski has obtained solid edge engagement.

Three exercises to help you practice the down stem are:

1 Ski across the slope in an open stance with flexed knees. Stem your downhill ski until you feel the edge grip. By setting the edge hard and building a platform in the snow, you can rebound into the traverse again. Do this a few times in sequence and you will make what is known as a down-stem garland.

2 Repeat the first exercise, but while stemming your downhill ski, turn your upper body in anticipation toward the fall line to give you that rebound feeling. (This rebound should bring you back to a traverse, but you are not as yet going to turn.)

3 Start out again, doing a traverse in the open stance. Stem your downhill ski and bend your downhill knee and move it inward, at the same time anticipating your upper body (by turning it to face the fall line) and planting your downhill pole. Stem, anticipation, and pole plant should occur almost simultaneously, and you will have to practice a lot before you can get your coordination right.

Now try to use the rebound you will get from the platform created by your downhill ski, quickly shifting your weight from it to the inner edge of your uphill ski. Your pole plant will assist this rebound action and help you to maintain balance during the transfer.

Anticipation

Anticipation, often called split-rotation, is the rotation of the upper body in the direction of a turn, prior to unweighting and edge set. It is used in short turns or in very sharp changes of direction. Slalom racers use it in tight turns, rotating their heads and bodies in the direction of the next turn in order to anticipate it.

If, wishing to turn while traversing, you turn your

(*ABOVE*) To do a down stem, you start out in a traverse in the open stance, keeping your knees flexed. (*1*) Stem your downhill ski and push your downhill knee into the hill to engage the inside edge of your ski hard. (*2*) Push off strongly from your downhill ski to transfer your weight to the turn's outside ski. Your outside leg then starts to turn, you change edges and begin to steer. (*3*) Match your inside ski after the stem to add to your turning motion. Steer through the rest of the turn.
(*LEFT*) The down stem as seen from behind.

upper body toward the fall line, supporting this movement by a firm pole plant, certain muscles in the lower back and hip area become stretched. When you relax those muscles, simultaneously retracting your legs quickly (thus releasing your edges), the muscles will "rebound" back to their normal position, causing your legs to return to the axis of your upper body, and your unweighted skis will twist in the direction of the next turn.

You can use anticipation in parallel turns with a check and when you make short-radius turns on steeper terrain. When using anticipation, your upper body will actually travel a shorter distance than your feet and skis.

Parallel Turns in the Open and Narrow Stance

What characterizes a parallel turn (often called a parallel christy) is that you keep your skis parallel throughout it. The parallel turn is the goal of most skiers. You should learn to perform smooth, controlled parallel turns in the open and narrow stance on all kinds of terrain and in all kinds of snow.

You initiate the turn from a run straight down the fall line. Turn to the right or left with a down motion, pivoting your legs in the direction of the turn. (In other words, an uphill christy off the fall line.) As you turn uphill from the fall line, you must shift your weight more to the outside ski. Before you come too square across the hill, discontinue the uphill christy by an up-unweighting movement in which you pivot both legs in the direction of the next turn, and initiate a new turn with a down motion of the body.

Parallel turns are easier to do close to the fall line. Aim at making the turns medium-sized by rhythmically raising and lowering the body and by using the legs to pivot the skis from side to side. Start your turns in the upright, natural position and finish them low, with a lot of pressure on the downhill ski. The steeper the terrain, the faster you will go, and the easier it will be to integrate a pole plant into your turns. Your poles will help you to stay in a natural, relaxed position and to initiate the up motion to start each turn. All advanced skiers use their poles when turning, particularly in shorter turns at slow and medium speed.

The more proficient you get at the parallel turn, the faster you will ski, and the more you should try to carve the turn instead of skidding through it.

Coordination

The only way to learn a new sport is to master its basics. Every sport has special demands, and to

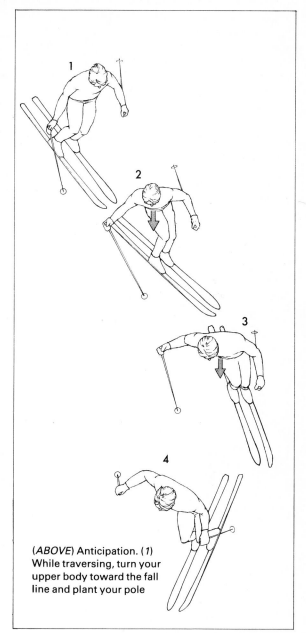

(*ABOVE*) Anticipation. (*1*) While traversing, turn your upper body toward the fall line and plant your pole

firmly. Most of your weight should be on your inside ski. (*2*) Lean your anticipated body into the turn while doing a check. (*3*) As you rebound, your skis are unweighted and will realign themselves with your body. (*4*) Steer through the turn.
(*LEFT*) When you use anticipation, your upper body (*1*) will travel a shorter distance than will your feet and skis (*2*). (*3*) Fall line.

85

meet them you must be familiar with them. This requires a lot of trial-and-error; the more experience you gain of the movements involved, the better you will become. Good instruction is important, it will lead you to correct practice. Coordination is simply being able to transfer into action what you have learned. Economy of movement is an important part of your coordination. Your body will perform according to how well you have learned the basic skills of the new sport. Coordination is the key to skiing, and the natural body position is fundamental in alpine skiing. When you can assume this position easily, you can properly balance your weight on your moving skis. By weighting and unweighting your skis, and tensing and relaxing your muscles, you will find that you tire less easily. This relaxation is necessary because the lower your position, the more strain you put on your muscles. Even the strongest skier will tire in the crouched position.

As you become more skilled, your reflexes will make you adapt "automatically" to the different conditions that arise on a slope—bumps and hollows, icy patches, etc.

(*BELOW*) You initiate a parallel turn from a run straight down the fall line. (*1*) Start doing an uphill christy off the fall line. As you turn uphill, shift your weight more to the outside ski. (*2*) Before your skis are too square across the hill, make a pole plant and an up-unweighting movement, during which you pivot both legs in the direction of the new turn. (*3*) Sink down to initiate the next turn.

(*ABOVE*) Linked parallel turns. The end of one turn is the beginning of the next.

86

5

THE ACCOMPLISHED SKIER

Snow conditions vary throughout the skiing season and, indeed, from day to day, depending on the weather conditions and the age of the snow. The daily change in temperature, wind, and amount and strength of sunshine cause varying snow conditions, some of which make for delightful skiing, while others are cordially detested by many skiers.

The skiing season itself varies from place to place. In parts of Europe, one can generally ski between November and mid-April, while other areas, such as parts of South America and Australia, have a skiing season from June to about September. And, of course, there are places where you can ski all the year round. The season can be shorter or longer, depending upon the amount and quality of the snow; these vary yearly.

Snow consists of precipitated ice crystals, which usually have a feathery or needle-like structure and which are formed from aqueous vapor in the atmosphere when the temperature is below freezing point. The crystals have a six-fold axis of symmetry and gather to form irregular snow flakes. The size and compactness of these flakes influence snow conditions. But the fall of snow is merely the beginning of a process in the snow cover; during this process, the newly fallen snow settles, shifts, melts, and freezes.

Today, we are able to aid this process with the help of machines that can groom and pack the snow on a slope; this does much to improve skiing conditions. Soft snow can be packed down to give a harder surface, while icy and crusty snow can be chopped up and repacked by special machinery.

Every snow field goes through certain basic changes during the season. In lower altitudes the snow can, for instance, melt, while in the higher altitudes it can consolidate into what is called firn, or névé, and eventually can turn into glacial ice. Powder snow is a general term for unsettled, freshly fallen snow with low density. Wild snow, which falls only in very cold weather with low air humidity, is a particular type of snow, and the term is applied to both the freshly fallen and the settled snow. In some parts of Europe during the winter nights, a peculiarly warm wind, the Föhn, may arise, which is able to melt a good part of the snow base overnight.

Snow consolidates mainly from its own weight. The tiny snow crystals are crushed, their minute projections are broken off, and the snow settles closer, leaving less air between the crystals. A powder-snow cover can soon develop a rain or sun crust. In the morning, this crust is crisp and crunchy; by the afternoon, it is soft and heavy, and has a high content of water, which can freeze at night. The in-between stage is a breakable crust that is not popular among some skiers. By noon in spring, a snow field with hard, dense snow has often turned soft and slushy. By evening, it can be hard again. As hard as this snow is, however, it should not be called ice. The term "ice" should be reserved for the green, blue, or blackish glass-like substance, patches of which can appear here and there on the slopes. On the lower slopes, the snow will melt away during the spring, but higher up, in the glacier areas above 8,200 feet (2,500 m), the temperature remains low all year round, and some of the snow will be retained, eventually turning into glacial ice. In glacial ice there is very little air between the ice crystals (some is trapped under high pressure in what is known as "bubble holes").

You may not always be happy about the snow conditions, but if you wait for the perfect day, you are not going to get much skiing done during the season! You will improve your technique by skiing in all kinds of snow, and this is the only way to finally become an expert skier. Remember that there are no really impossible snow conditions, only less skilled skiers!

Skiing on Ice or Icy Snow

Many people get nervous and lose confidence if they hear that conditions are icy. They often panic on the slopes, forget the hard-learned basics, and exaggerate their movements in order to keep their balance. Nothing could be more wrong.

Hard-packed snow and ice are found mostly on heavily trafficked slopes where thousands of people ski all day long. After some days, the surface of such a slope becomes hard as cement, and after a day of warmer weather, ice will form as soon as the temperature drops below freezing point. Ice may affect an entire slope or only form in patches where shadows have prevented the sun from thawing the snow during the day. A patch of ice may be unexpected, but it should not take you by surprise if you keep your eyes open and on the slope in front of you. You will find ice in the shade, or where everybody makes the same turn, or on the downhill side of a mogul, where the snow has been badly scraped by numerous skiers. Sometimes, there can be a natural spring in the side of a slope, and areas flooded by its water will freeze and show up as greenish or bluish spots. During your first few runs on the slope, you will see these spots; after that, you should simply avoid them.

Skiing on ice makes special demands on your

equipment and your technique. Your skis must be in good shape and have sharp edges and flat bases. A few minutes' work on the skis before you go on ice will be well worth the effort. Flat-file the running surfaces so that the bottoms of the edges are flush with the base, and side-file the edges (especially the inner edges) to make them really sharp (keep that angle at 90°). See Chapter Two for details on how to do this. As is also pointed out in Chapter Two, your boots must be stiff and well-fitting, so that your steering movements are immediately transmitted to your skis.

Almost anybody can ski on soft snow, where it is easy to cheat, but ice demands correct, flowing technique. Most average skiers get into trouble on ice because they cannot ski correctly.

The secret of skiing on ice is a certain feeling for movement—neither too much nor too little, neither too fast nor too slow; just smooth, effortless movement. Don't get tense, and don't fight the ice. Beginners should avoid trying to turn on ice, but should turn before they hit it or else cross it and turn in the crisp snow on the other side. Advanced skiers who master the technique of carving a turn by steering with the knees can carve a turn on ice as long as they keep their movements smooth and their skis in contact with the ice and snow.

Some points to remember when skiing on ice:

1 Don't use your upper body to initiate a turn. If you do this, you can lose your smoothness of movement and you will be delayed in getting your edges to work.

2 Keep your center of gravity over your boots. If you allow it to drop behind your boots, you lose control as soon as you hit ice, since the speed of your skis will increase, giving you no chance to regain your balance.

3 When traversing, keep more weight on the inside edge of your downhill ski than on the uphill ski. This should be done to the outside ski when you are turning.

4 When planting your poles, don't push yourself forward; sink down instead, thus keeping your center of gravity over your boots.

5 When doing stem turns on ice, feel the inside edge of your outside ski, and gradually but firmly shift your weight onto it.

6 In parallel turns, assume a pronounced comma, or angulated, position, so that as much weight as possible goes over to the outside ski, as you gradually increase the amount of edge hold on that ski. The edge will bite into the ice and hold you smoothly through the turn. Too much pressure on the edge can sometimes make the ski "chatter."

7 The radius of your turns will be much wider on ice than on soft snow. Keep this in mind, especially if there are many other skiers on the slope.

8 Learn to take the ice in your stride and use it to your advantage. After having skied through a period during which the snow has been icy, you will feel more confident when skiing good snow again, because you will have developed a better feeling for exact timing and for good economy of movement.

Skiing on Heavy Snow

At the end of the skiing season, the rising temperature causes a change in the snow conditions, and the skier is confronted with wet, heavy, sticky snow, often called crud, or junk, snow. The average skier may find this kind of snow difficult and even dangerous to ski on; it requires experience and physical fitness. It arises when evaporation, air humidity, wind, sun, and the high water content of the snow itself cause the snow crystals to adhere to one another and to the bottoms of the skis. That is when the skier feels that he cannot turn because his skis just will not slide. The ski tips tend to sink into the snow instead of planing on it; waxing is now more needed than ever. You also need a shorter, wider, and softer ski in this type of snow.

Developing a good heavy-snow technique is very similar to starting the basics again.

1 Keep your skis equally weighted and parallel.

2 Put more weight on your heels, so that the ski tips do not sink in the snow. Edge control should then be no problem.

3 Your unweighting technique is very important. The up–down movement caused by flexing knees and ankles must be exaggerated, but the movement should be limited to the legs and not involve the upper body. Don't bend over from the waist, as this will bury your ski tips in the snow and cause you to fall forward.

4 Try to ski in the fall line; the resistance is less there. Also, the higher speed you will attain will help you force your skis through the snow.

If you want to practice these fundamentals, try a gentle slope for a few straight runs and traverses, with both skis equally weighted. Practice unweighting and use your poles to give you rhythm and timing. Make sure your hands stay in front of you at their respective sides. From a traverse, try an uphill christy, using the up–down movement (unweighting), as described above. Try to initiate the turning of the skis by rotating your hips. This will cause your ski tails to slide downhill, while the tips twist uphill. Because of the extreme resistance

outward and downhill a bit. (*3*) Continue turning during the down part of the up–down movement, pivoting both legs. It will help if you lean your body slightly inward. (*4*) Initiate the next turn by unweighting and by starting to rotate the hips again.

(*ABOVE*) Skiing on heavy snow requires parallel and evenly weighted skis, with more weight than normal on the heels.
(*ABOVE RIGHT*) Turning in heavy snow. (*1*) In a steep traverse, unweight your skis with an up–down movement from the legs. Don't bend forward from the waist. (*2*) Initiate the turn by rotating your hips at the end of the up part of the up–down movement. Your ski tails will now skid

of heavy snow, you will sometimes need to rotate your upper body to initiate or complete a turn. Initiate the turn at the end of an up motion; your skis will then be unweighted and easier to turn.

To turn your skis into the fall line from a traverse, unweight them by lifting, turn, and then sink down again. After a few tries, you will have enough confidence to link a right and a left turn. Stay as close as you can to the fall line.

If your parallel turns are a bit sloppy, try doing the turns with an up stem (page 82). Stem to the fall line and finish the turn while matching your skis (this can be very tricky in crud). Carry out all movements without hesitation and always keep some weight on both skis (never balance completely on one ski).

When making a parallel turn down the fall line in crud snow, always keep both skis equally weighted and try to keep up as high a speed as possible. Turn your skis while they are unweighted, and use a pole plant to aid the lifting motion. The turning power should come from the hips and the legs, with the upper body and arms following the turn.

It is never easy to ski on crud snow, and even the best skier will have problems in adjusting to it. But those who still wish to develop as skiers and to ski until the end of the season, when this type of snow is usually found, should, with a lot of practice, be able to handle crud snow.

How to Ski on Steep Terrain

Very often, you will find steep spots in a descent. These are known as head walls, and inexperienced skiers are frequently afraid to try them out. Accomplished skiers, far from avoiding them, seek them out for the challenge and the workout they provide. Here the skier cannot get away with cheating.

On steep slopes, the pole plant before turning is very important, as it gives you timing and balance. The pole acts as the pivot round which you make the turn. Again, the pole plant should come out of the wrist and, mainly, should be a mere touch

(*ABOVE*) Tracks made by a skidded (*1*) and a carved (*2*) turn.
(*BELOW*) A carved turn can be made either with the skis' fronts (*1*) or tails (*2*). When carving with the fronts, push your knees forward and into the turn.

When carving with the tails, don't rotate your knees into the turn so much, but weight your heels more as you finish the turn.

(although at times it must take some of your weight). Your stance should be lower than the natural position, your knees and ankles being more flexed than on a gentle slope. This is necessary if you are to get a proper edge-set in order to build a platform for your push-off into the coming turn. The kind of turn you are making will decide how close you should keep your arms, and it will also dictate the position of your upper body. You need lots of knee angulation, as well as some hip angulation; this causes edging, and edging is what you use to control speed. When you are skiing short-radius turns, your upper body should face straight down the fall line, whereas it should follow the turns when you are skiing wide-radius turns. To prepare for unweighting, when the edges are set, extend your arm forward and downhill and plant your pole. Your knees should be well flexed and the pole should carry some of your weight when you push off from the platform, quickly swinging your skis across the fall line, and setting an aggressive edge. When your skis hit the snow again, the downhill pole should be ready to be planted once more.

Carving Turns of Various Sizes

All skiing turns can be either skidded or carved. Carving is the art of reducing lateral sideslip throughout the turn (the theoretically perfect carved turn has no sideslip) in an attempt to ski the arc produced by bending and edging the ski and pressing it into the snow. In a carved turn, the snow's resistance along the entire edge of the ski is the main cause of the ski's turning. A skidded turn, on the other hand, is initiated and controlled by muscular turning forces (rotation and counter-rotation).

The advanced skier uses the natural characteristics of a well-designed ski which, when weighted and edged correctly, will turn in a curved path without skidding. An active fore and aft weight transfer, combined with the edge bite exerted by the muscles that control the angulation of the lower body, is used to steer the skis through the turn.

There are two ways of carving a turn. You can carve it with the front of the ski by pushing the knee forward and turning it in the direction of the turn, thus putting more pressure on the front and the shovel of the ski. And you can do it with the tails of your skis, so you do not need so much knee angulation. As you finish your turn, transfer more weight to your heels by moving your center of gravity backward.

Skiing in Powder and Untracked Snow

Skiing in deep snow is one of the most exciting and exhilarating experiences a skier can have. However, the fact that you are a good packed-snow skier does not automatically mean that you will immediately feel comfortable the first time you try skiing in deep powder and untracked snow. If you use the proper technique, you will find that the powder snow provides a fairly solid platform for your skis.

Skiing in up to a foot (30 cm) of powder snow on a base of packed snow requires no change in your skiing technique. All you have to do is to get used to skiing without being able to see your skis. But as the snow gets deeper, you must adjust your technique to the conditions by, for instance, putting more weight on the heels of your boots so that the tips tend to come up toward the surface.

When skiing on untracked snow, don't go alone. Skiing on your own can be very dangerous, as bad weather or avalanches can surprise you.

Parallel Turns in Deep Powder

Parallel turns in deep powder require a refinement of the technique that has first been learned on well-packed slopes. You need quick reflexes, good physical condition, and no fear of speed. In a normal parallel turn on a well-packed slope (page 86), you have most of your weight on the downhill ski, but in deep powder, you must distribute your weight evenly between the skis. Another refinement of the normal parallel turn that makes it possible for you to turn in deep powder is an exaggerated down–up–down motion. In the down part you must keep your upper body upright while flexing your knees and hips so that you put more weight on your heels, thus causing the tips of your skis to surface from beneath the snow. Now stretch into the up motion, gradually pushing your hip sideways into the turn. Depending on how deep the powder is, plant your downhill pole firmly to give yourself a push-off at the same time as you stretch up. However, if the powder is deep, then the pole plant will be no more than a gesture, but it is useful from the point of view of rhythm. As you push your hip sideways into the turn, your unweighted skis will turn near the surface of the snow. Now sink down gradually with your weight distributed evenly between the skis, until you "feel" the underneath surface. This down motion is the first part of your next parallel turn. Throughout your run, keep your knees and feet close together, and ski close to the fall line.

After some practice, you can increase your speed

Short parallel turns in deep powder call for evenly weighted skis and a narrow stance. Stay close to the fall line. (*1*) Stretch your legs sideways until you have built up resistance under your skis. (*2*) Plant your downhill pole and retract your legs so that your skis are under your body. (*3*) Pivot your unweighted skis into the new turn and stretch your legs sideways. This will reset the edges, while the pressure on the skis will make them go into reverse camber. Keep your weight mainly on your heels during the turn. (*4*) When your legs are outstretched, retract your skis again and start the next turn. A light pole plant and anticipation will help the pivoting movement.

and control the radius of your turns better. This will enable you to ski more rhythmically and to make short-radius turns.

Skiing through Gates

Probably you have already tried skiing through some slalom gates when you were practicing your wedge turn and gliding wedge (Chapter Three), and you will have realized that there is a big difference between free skiing and running the gates, as skiing through gates is called. To be able to run the gates the way the top skiers do it, you must master all the turns, movements, and positions already covered in this book (especially carving, edging, step turns, angulation, and anticipation).

Start with easy combinations set up in the fall line on a fairly easy slope. When you have mastered this course, move to a more difficult course on steeper terrain, where you will automatically get up more speed when skiing in the fall line. On this course, you will be able to increase the pressure on the edge of your downhill ski in order to turn from the fall line. To get back over the fall line you must use a step turn.

When you have accustomed yourself to this, try your hand at a short course—about ten gates should be sufficient—in which you must make wide-radius, giant-slalom turns. As yet, it is unnecessary to try skiing close to the inner poles of the gates. The important thing is that you develop the proper sense of timing and that you learn to start your turns early enough.

Short-swing Turn with Check

Short-swing turns are linked, short-radius parallel christies, preceded by a check and performed with the aid of pole plants. The pole plants help the skier find the correct rhythm and also tell him when to start the unweighting motion necessary to initiate the following turn—there are no traverses between the turns. Short-swing turns are easier to learn if you use skis which are shorter than those you normally use and if you ski with an open stance.

On an averagely steep slope, you don't need to turn your skis too much. Start out in a steep traverse and increase your angulation as you prepare for the pole plant. Your upper body should be facing downhill all through the edge set and the turn. Push your knees downhill to flatten your skis and begin to sideslip, thrusting the tails of your skis downhill with your heels. After a short sideslip, push your knees into the slope to re-set your edges, making them bite hard. This checking movement will cause you to flex your knees more.

You will find it easier to learn short-swing turns if you ski with an open stance and use somewhat shorter skis than normally. (*1*) Start out on a steep hill in a traverse and increase your angulation. Keep your upper body facing the fall line all through the turn. (*2*) Push your knees outward and downhill until you begin to sideslip. At the same time, thrust the tails of your skis outward and downward. After a short sideslip, you forcefully set your edges; you will then automatically flex your knees more and increase your angulation even further. Just as your edges bite hard, plant your downhill pole, start the up-motion, and push off against the snow under your skis. (*3*) When your skis are unweighted, they will automatically be turned toward the fall line, since your upper body faces downhill. Continue this turning with your feet, and steer with your knees through the turn. As soon as you have re-set your edges, you will be ready to start the next turn.

As the edges bite and just before you start the up motion, plant your downhill pole and push off from the "platform" of snow under your skis. Since your upper body is facing downhill and thus anticipated, the rebound from your stretched muscles will turn your skis toward the fall line automatically when they are unweighted. Complete the turn by steering with your knees.

As you become more experienced, you will find your movements getting smoother, and you will be using only your legs when pushing off, while your torso stays "quiet" throughout the turn. By then, your turns and edge changes will have become faster and more precise.

The more or less aggressive checks you do be-tween the turns permit you to go much slower down a steep slope than would be possible if you used a series of linked traverses or long-radius parallel turns. Short-swing turns are mostly used on very steep, icy terrain where a too-fast descent can be braked by means of the aggressive edge set. Your upper body should face the fall line all the time and should remain almost motionless—its counter-rotation should only be sufficient to balance out the twisting of your lower body. (Counter-rotation is the motion of the upper body when it rotates in the opposite direction to the lower body.) As has already been mentioned, the short-swing turn is a braking turn which leads to the ski tails' moving in a sweeping way from side

The wedel is skied rhythmically in a narrow stance. Your upper body should face the fall line all through the turns. (*1*) Sink down and forward by flexing your knees, and pull your feet and legs up slightly under you. Plant the downhill pole at the end of the down movement, and start straightening your body (*2*), during which movement you stretch your legs and (*3*) sweep the ski tails out to one side. (*4*) Set the edges smoothly. Pull your legs and skis back in and under you and plant your pole. You are now ready to start the straightening movement, during which you sweep your ski tails out to the other side.

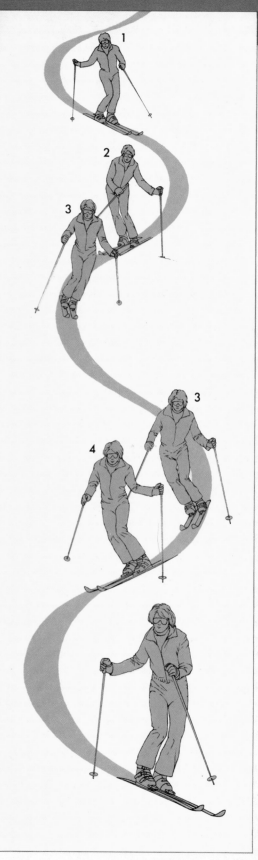

to side while the skier's upper body faces the fall line and moves more directly downhill.

The Classic Wedel

It is fascinating to watch good skiers "dance" down a slope doing wedel turns. The wedel is little more than linked parallel turns without traverses and with very little edge set that can check the speed. The difference between the wedel and the short-swing turn is that the latter has a more vigorous edge set, which causes checking. The wedel is performed on almost flat skis, the tails being swept from side to side by leg action. The result is a smooth, flowing, snake-like motion in which the end of one turn is the beginning of the next, and all movements are done rhythmically. During the wedel, the upper body should remain almost motionless, both laterally and vertically, and it acts as a stabilizer for the leg movement. All the action comes from the hips, knees, and ankles, while the upper body always faces down the fall line. The arms and hands stay in front and to the sides, and the poles are planted with a minimum of hand and arm movement, the action originating in the wrist.

In the steering phases, mistakes do not matter too much, because, as your hips and knees move your skis from side to side over the fall line, you will not have the time to turn the mass of your torso. If you plant your pole when starting the next turn, the pole plant will act as a brake on that side of your body. To this counter-force you add the turning force of the legs, which is the main source of turning power.

The classic wedel is a flowing series of turns, each of which is initiated by a slight down–up movement in which you flex your knees, bringing your feet up under you. This unweights the skis and allows you to sweep the ski tails out to one side by stretching your legs. Plant the outside pole lightly (to help you maintain rhythm) and set the edges smoothly. Now pull your skis back in and up under you before pushing them away from you and out to the other side, all in one flowing movement. Keep your weight mostly on the outside ski and shift the same amount of weight for each turn, so that your tracks are symmetrical and you have a good rhythm.

Circling bumps in a mogul field rather than crossing them might sound like the easiest way out, but it is actually very difficult, as you must turn very quickly each time and there is always a risk of catching your tips or tails.

To control your speed, make the turn rounder by sweeping out the tails more.

Points to remember when skiing wedel turns.

1 Keep your upper body facing down the fall line. Look where you are going, not at your skis.

2 Don't rotate your upper body, as this will cause you to turn too far.

3 Keep your hands in front of you, at their respective sides.

4 The pole plant should come out of your wrist. Plant a pole for each turn and do it at the end of the down part of the unweighting movement.

5 Keep your knees and skis together, so that the skis act as a single unit.

6 Do not push your ski tails out too far from the fall line.

Skiing Moguls

When you look up a frequently used slope, you can see moguls, that is, hummocks that have been built up as a result of the constant turning of many skiers on the same spot. A good mogul field should look like a slalom course. Many skiers do their best to avoid mogul fields, however, since they feel that they cannot master them, but once you have learned how, you will find skiing moguls to be a lot of fun.

There are two ways of dealing with moguls. You either go round them or you go over them. In practice, you use a combination of these ways. If you ski round the moguls, following the troughs, it will be like running a slalom course. Your route and turns will be wholly determined by the mogul field,

To ski a big mogul at high speed, use avalement (active retraction to absorb the bump). (*1*) Approach the mogul in a relaxed, upright stance. (*2*) Use anticipation, plant your pole, and pull your thighs up under you, at the same time as you shoot your feet forward and upward. Edge and weight your outside ski. (*3*) As you go over the top, stretch your legs out and down. Continue the turn by edging the outside ski more and steer by pivoting the outside ski while you stretch your body in preparation for the next turn.

and all you have to do is to adapt to the terrain and follow the given track. This is, in fact, very difficult, as you must be able to turn very fast, and even then there is a chance of your catching your tips or tails between the moguls. A better way—and the more challenging—is to go over the top. There are two important elements in skiing moguls in this way: absorption and making the turn at the top of the bump. You must be able to absorb the shock from the sudden elevation of the mogul, and this absorption·takes place in the legs. Approach the mogul with alert yet relaxed muscles. If the mogul is slight, then relaxed legs are enough to allow the rising face of the mogul to push your legs, flexed at the knees and the ankles, upward, thus absorbing the shock and allowing your shoulders to keep more or less at the same level throughout the maneuver, thus helping you to retain balance.

As you become experienced at skiing moguls, you will want to tackle the big ones—and at higher speeds. This means that you are going to hit the mogul harder, so your reaction must be stronger and faster. To increase shock absorption, retract your legs, flexing them sharply at the knees, hips, and ankles. When you get to the top of the bump,

your tails and tips will be off the snow, the only point of contact being under your boots. There will now be no problem in turning your skis in the right direction. Plant your downhill pole, and as soon as you go over the top, stretch your legs out to regain contact with the snow. You can now front sideslip down the face of the mogul, preparing yourself for the next turn; however, it is better if you can carve or steer the sideslip into the next turn.

Christy with Reploiement

As you arrive at the foot of a mogul, adopt a fairly upright position and, as you feel the ground rise, let your legs absorb it (this is reploiement). Simultaneously, face your upper body down the fall line in anticipation. When at the top, plant your downhill pole, pivot your skis, and stretch your legs, and you will follow the turn of the skis. Your upper body is now in alignment with your legs, and you prepare for the next turn.

Christy with Avalement

Avalement is the movement that changes the body from a fairly upright position to the compressed, crouched position necessary when you go over a

(*OPPOSITE*) A mogul field at Tignes.
(*RIGHT*) Start the jet turn in a steep traverse, with your hips, knees, and ankles somewhat flexed. (*1*) Sink down and set your edges hard (keep your center of gravity over your heels) as you plant your pole and anticipate your upper body markedly. (*2*) When the eges bite, the skis go into reverse camber, storing kinetic energy, and you can pull your legs up under you. (*3*) Your upper body will now move forward and downward in the direction of the coming turn, and your feet will be "pushed" obliquely forward and upward. When the skis are unweighted in this manner, they will be swung toward the fall line and into the new turn, and their edges change. (*4*) Steer through the turn by varying the edge-set of your outside ski and by using your legs.

big mogul at high speed. In avalement you contract your stomach muscles rapidly, retract your legs hard, and shoot your feet forward. This jack-knifing action enables you to "swallow" the mogul with your legs and, combined with anticipation, tips the upper body slightly forward and downhill. The forward projection of your feet helps you to keep contact with the snow during the rest of the turn, and to retain the relaxed, fairly upright position you need for tackling the next mogul.

The stages of the christy with avalement are the following. As you make contact with the face of the mogul, you are in a relaxed, fairly upright position. In a flowing, uninterrupted movement, you prepare the turn by anticipation, a downhill pole plant, and by pulling your thighs up under you. At the same time, you shoot your feet forward and upward (this is known as the pre-turn). The turn is initiated by edging and weighting the outside ski. As you go down the other side of the mogul, your feet and skis seek contact with the snow, so you stretch your legs outward and downward. Steer the turn by leg rotation and edging, as you extend your body to the natural, fairly upright position, in preparation for the next turn.

Jet Turns

To ski jet turns, you use an advanced skiing technique with a quick edge change and a weight transfer at the initiation of each turn. In many ways, the jet turn is similar to the rebound, but there are some vital differences. Simplified, a rebound can be described as a rapid, hard-biting edge set that results in a platform from which you can push off but that also brakes the forward motion in the face of the coming weight shift and the release of the turn. You push off by partly stretching your legs, and the motion becomes an upward–forward one in the direction of what will be the new turn. In a jet turn, however, you try deliberately to avoid, or at least soften down, the braking effect of the edge bite. This you do partly by exaggerating anticipation and partly by firmly keeping your center of gravity over your heels at the very moment you edge your skis.

As soon as the edges bite, the skis go into reverse camber (because of the abrupt edge set), and you pull your thighs up by contracting your abdominal and hip-lifting muscles. Your upper body, which has been blocked by a determined pole plant, simultaneously moves forward and downward in the direction of the imminent turn. Since your ankles and lower legs are relaxed, the built-in resilience of the skis will give your feet and skis a "push" in an oblique forward-and-upward direction—the jet motion. Since the skis are not weighted at this very moment, your feet and skis swing automatically toward the fall line and into the new turn (due to the anticipation of your upper body).

The Parallel Step Turn, or Lateral Projection

If you have just completed a turn and are in a somewhat crouched position, with most of the pressure on your outside (downhill) ski, which is edged, you can gain height in preparation for the next turn by using a parallel step turn.

What you must do is to stretch your outside leg forward and uphill (a kind of push-off), while you lift the inside, unweighted ski uphill. (The inside ski will also move forward, as you are moving forward.) As you are stepping with the unweighted ski, that is, while it is in the air, change its edge, and as you put it down, transfer your weight to it. This ski will be the outside ski of the next turn. The turn is now steered as usual, with more or less parallel skis that are more or less edged (depending on whether you are carving or skidding the turn).

Remember that in the parallel step turn, the edge change takes place in the air, while the turn is effected on the snow. The push-off and the radius of the turns must be adjusted to each other. If you push off too much from the lower ski, you will turn too late; if you push off too little, you will need very much twisting force to turn the skis. Keep your weight over the middle of the skis and weight the entire outside ski along its inner edge. This will give you a good platform from which you can push off.

The parallel step turn is used for quickly changing edges on the outside ski of a new turn, for getting a better line through a turn, and even to gain height before a new turn. (*1*) Having completed a turn, ski in a somewhat crouched position with most of your weight on the outside ski's inner edge. (*2*) Push away forward and upward by stretching your outside leg, and move the inner unweighted ski uphill, changing its edges and turning it into the new turn

Alpine Ski Touring

People who enjoy the beauty of snow-clad mountains and like to be the first to ski on untracked snow are truly missing something special if they do not try alpine ski touring. The number of lifts and cable cars has increased so much that there is hardly any mountain in the vicinity of densely populated areas that is not crowded with skiers every weekend. This is one of the reasons why more and more people go in for alpine ski touring. Most of them are looking for recreation in a beautiful, quiet countryside and a feeling of freedom—in short, they want to get away from the hustle and bustle of everyday life, and that is hardly possible on a crowded slope with tremendous waiting lines at the ski lifts.

The northern European and the Alpine countries are famous for their alpine ski touring. Many well-known mountains are only reachable on skis by people who enjoy the sport, appreciate the beauty of the surroundings, and do not hesitate to exert themselves. These people pack their rucksacks, put on their alpine-touring equipment, and set off up the mountains, while others may have to wait for hours in crowded ski resorts for a chance to ski. Each alpine ski tour has its particular challenge and reward—you will come across different fields, woods, trails, rivers, mountains, animals—all the beauties and wonders of nature.

Taking up alpine ski touring does not mean that

while it is in the air. (*3*) As soon as the uphill ski's inside edge bites, increase pressure on it. (*4*) Steer through the turn as usual by adjusting edge-set and by sinking down to put pressure on the outside ski.

you have to give up all other types of skiing, but it does make a very exciting change. Above all, it makes you totally independent. You can start early in the morning, driving out of the city to start your tour by skiing through fields and woods, along trickling streams and on lonely trails into high valleys. You have to find your own way up the mountains, for everything is covered with virgin snow. If you are out early enough, you will be able to reach the top of a mountain in time to see the sunrise—a spectacular sight.

Naturally, in alpine ski touring, you have only one run down the mountain. Then you have to climb it—or some other mountain—all over again. But you are able to enjoy skiing up the mountain, too, admiring the beauty of the surrounding peaks and delighting in the pleasure of setting your tracks into virgin snow. To some people, this can be much more exciting than waiting in lift lines and skiing down the same slope ten or twenty times a day.

Before you can go alpine ski touring, you have to be a very good skier, but apart from that, you must know how to read a map and how to use a compass, so that you do not get lost. Always check the weather forecast and the snow conditions for the area before setting out, and check especially whether there is any risk of avalanches or snow storms; both are hazards which are best avoided. Pack your rucksack with everything you might need in case of bad weather, for weather reports are not always sufficiently accurate and detailed, and the local weather in the mountains can change very rapidly—from clear skies and brilliant sun-

shine to thick fog and falling snow in less than an hour. Always prepare your alpine ski tours well in advance. The mountains can be dangerous, especially for those without enough knowledge and experience.

In a way, alpine ski touring is similar to cross-country skiing, but in alpine ski touring, you climb up to the tops of mountains, whereas the cross-country skier stays in the valleys, skiing more or less at the same level all the time. Further, the equipment required for alpine ski touring differs from that used for cross-country skiing.

The basic equipment for alpine ski touring is a shorter (160–180 cm or 63–71 inches), wider, and softer ski than the usual downhill ski, and a special touring binding, which allows you to lift your heel

The above series of pictures shows how a powder avalanche is triggered off by a skier and how it gets wider and wider on its way down the slope. The airy powder snow slides downhill very rapidly and with almost no friction between it and the rest of the snow. By the way, the skier made it—this time . . .

The avalanche shown is known as a surface avalanche, and it occurs because powder snow has a weak bond between its crystals. Another type of surface avalanche is the

wet-snow avalanche, which rolls more slowly but is no less dangerous for that. If the entire layer of snow breaks away, the slip is known as a fall depth avalanche. Slab avalanches are characterized by a cleavage in the snow at the point where the avalanche is triggered off. An avalanche can start for several reasons. Important factors are the gradient of the hill, the consistency of the snow, the wind, and the temperature.

The best way to avoid avalanches is, of course,

not to ski off prepared slopes. Second best is to learn which conditions and which types of terrain constitute avalanche risks and then to avoid dangerous slopes. If you do want to ski off-piste and, understandably, many do, as off-piste skiing provides the greatest challenge and the most fun for the expert skier, then consult the local inhabitants and check if there have been avalanche warnings. Never ski downhill in a tight-knit group; keep your distance! Then, if anything happens, you will not all be caught by the avalanche, and, as happened in the pictures above, your friends can dig you out.

from the ski while you climb up the mountains but which can be locked to immobilize your heel for the downhill run. Without this ability to lift the heel from the ski, you would become very tired while climbing, and you would probably blister your heels badly. The toe, however, must be firmly attached to the ski, so that you can guide it properly. There are many different makes of touring bindings on the market, and any of them will do the job. You will also need a pair of longer-than-normal poles with rather large baskets to give you enough support in soft snow. To be able to ski uphill without sliding backward, you need climbing skins for the skis. Climbing skins used to be made of sea-lion skin, but nowadays, they are mostly made of synthetic cloth, such as plush. A pair of

good touring boots, which are neither as high nor as stiff as ordinary downhill ski boots, are also required. However, the boot soles must be stiff, otherwise the bindings will not work properly. Further, you will need woolen (or similar) socks, gloves, knickerbockers, sweaters, a wind-breaking jacket and ditto slacks, warm head-gear, sun glasses or goggles, a raincoat (in case of a change in the weather), food, drink, maps, a compass, and a good rucksack to carry your things in. Never go on an alpine ski tour without a complete first-aid kit and a repair kit for equipment and clothing (screwdriver, pliers, copper wire and nails, spare parts for bindings, needle and thread, nylon twine, screws, nails, etc.).

If you are going to tour a glacial region, you will also need at least 40 m (44 yards) of 9-mm ($\frac{3}{8}$ inch) thick nylon climbing rope for every two of you, ice axes, crampons, and carabines.

There is no special technique designed for alpine ski touring; you simply slide your skis forward when on uphill terrain and ski downhill as usual, but a good knowledge of the terrain and a sharp look-out for dangers when going up and skiing down are essential, as is a good "feeling" for the condition of the snow. Always look for the easiest and safest way of getting up or down a mountain.

(OPPOSITE) For some people, alpine touring is more than just skiing—it's a way of life.
(BELOW) This binding is specially designed for alpine touring. (1) It uncatches to allow the heel vertical freedom when climbing. (2) When fastened down, it holds the heel firmly in place for downhill skiing.

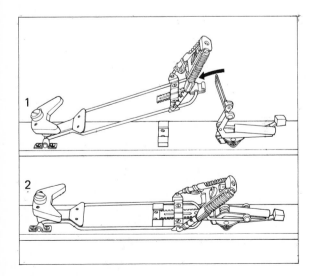

While on your way up, examine the terrain to find a suitable way down. Don't try to go straight uphill, as this will tire you out. Going in traverses will conserve energy and strength. Be extra careful when you happen on very steep; it is always a better choice to turn and find a safer route, and this is nearly always possible. But if you have to cross a potentially dangerous snow field, you and your companions (never go alpine skiing alone) should do so one at a time while the rest of the party carefully watch the moving skier. If he triggers an avalanche and gets buried by it, the others can attempt to dig him out or, should this fail, they can mark the spot where the skier was last seen and go raise the alarm, so that a rescue team will organize a search.

Safety first! Always think about possible risks before doing anything up in the mountains. Far too many people have already lost their lives in the mountains, and the number unfortunately grows each year, since too many inexperienced people with poor equipment are getting themselves into risky situations.

If you go up to glacial regions, you will face the danger of crevasses. Never cross a snow-covered glacier without a rope tied between yourself and at least one companion. Many people have been killed because they were not aware of the existence of crevasses or because they thought they knew where all the crevasses were. Always study the terrain you intend to cross, and do it very carefully. In late spring and early summer, most of the crevasses will still be covered with snow, but the snow may well no longer be able to hold your weight. This is why you should always be attached by a rope to at least one other person. A good team would consist of at least three people. Then, if one falls down a crevasse, the other two can help him out of trouble by fixing the rope next to the crevasse with an ice axe. Unless he is badly hurt, the person in the crevasse will then be able to climb out. Otherwise, one of his companions will have to climb down and bring him up.

It is a wonderful reward to reach the top of a mountain when the weather is clear and sunny. You can then enjoy the beautiful view in peace and quiet while you eat your lunch and plan the descent along a route you decided on while going uphill. It is important to really plan the descent in detail, so that you do not ski into steep, rocky, or otherwise dangerous terrain. If the ascent was safe, you should try to stay close to the tracks you made on the way up. You should then be able to ski safely back into the valley from which you set out.

Freestyle Skiing

Freestyle skiing has become very popular during the last few years. Many people believe that learning it is something only elite skiers can do, but that is not so—any good allround skier can do it. What you need is good coordination, well-adjusted safety bindings, and good judgment. Freestyle skiing can be a challenge, since it is a different and demanding way of skiing down a slope. Of course, freestyle skiing is not for everyone, but anyone who feels tempted should give it a try. You will find out soon enough whether you like it or not.

The first thing you should be concerned about when learning freestyle is your general skiing ability. You should be a good enough skier to be able to correct the mistakes you are bound to make while learning. You must pay a great deal of attention to your technique when starting to practice freestyle and concentrate on doing things right. Otherwise, freestyle practice can lead to stiff and uncoordinated skiing. When correctly performed, however, freestyle will help you improve your coordination even further.

Remember, though, that some freestyle stunts can be dangerous to others as well as to yourself if done on a crowded slope. So don't. Look for a hill which has been set aside for freestyle practice.

Today, most ski schools have accepted freestyle and frequently teach their students some of the freestyle tricks as an integrated part of the ordinary course programs. There are, of course, also courses in which freestyle only is taught, and the more daring stunts should always be learned at a ski school.

A good freestyle skier exhibits rhythm, elegance, and controlled dynamics. The freestyle competition program is divided into three disciplines: stunt and ballet skiing, mogul skiing, and aerial acrobatics.

Stunt and ballet skiing consists of dancing turns and steps, performed with rhythm and creative elegance on a gentle, mogul-free slope. The sources of inspiration for this type of freestyle skiing are figure skating and ordinary ballet.

Mogul skiing is the type of freestyle skiing which is closest to traditional alpine skiing. In Europe, this discipline is often called "hotdog skiing," a term which, in the United States, is synonymous with "freestyle skiing." Mogul skiing is for those advanced general skiers who can easily turn their skis, no matter how difficult or steep the terrain. A run through the bumps of a mogul field is a pleasure for such skiers—wild, exciting, without rules,

(*LEFT*) Hand in hand, two freestyle skiers are doing a straight back somersault in layout position.
(*ABOVE*) A front somersault in the tuck position.

but under complete control. Speed, elegance, and balance between moguls is what it's all about. In a skiing area, there are nearly always some runs which cannot be groomed because they are too steep for the machinery. Such runs are often reserved for the mogul skiers, and they will usually be there, buggying the bumps.

The last type of freestyle skiing, aerial acrobatics, is the most difficult and dangerous of all. It consists of different jumps—anything from an easy spread-eagle to an acrobatic flip—over moguls or well-prepared jumps, and the very best jumpers are usually gymnasts or divers. This type of freestyle skiing certainly is not for everyone; besides, even if performed by a person wearing skis, flips through the air can hardly be classified as skiing. Anyone who tries to do aerial acrobatics with skis on should have practiced the jumps to perfection from a trampoline in a gym or swimming pool before going out on the snow. As easy as some of the jumps look, they are difficult to learn, and accidents happen even to the best. Ordinary jumps, however, which the skier performs in a more or less upright position, taking off from the top of a bump in the terrain while going downhill, have always been a natural part of alpine skiing. Such jumps train the skier's coordination, balance, power of judgment and courage.

Most of the freestyle techniques described below can be practiced with ordinary alpine ski equipment. Freestyle experts, however, use fairly short skis (63–71 inches or 160–180 cm) for stunt and ballet skiing, since shorter skis are easier to turn than are long ones. A 4-inch (10 cm) reduction in the length of the skis will save fifteen percent of the energy needed to turn them. For the other types of freestyle skiing, up to 79 inches (200 cm) long skis are used, since these give better stability.

Stunt and Ballet Skiing

Ballet consists of lots of different movements and figures which can be combined at will, and they are often performed to music. The result should look like a very elegant and spectacular dance on snow.

One of the basic techniques is skiing on what is otherwise considered to be the wrong ski, that is, the inside ski of the turn. This has to be mastered first, as it is one of the fundamental steps to the different ballet figures.

A few exercises will help your balance. Try these on a gentle slope:

1 Balance on one ski while going down the fall line.

2 Put a few skating steps together, balancing as

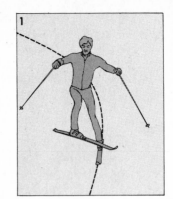

long as you can on the weighted ski after each push-off.

3 Do exercise number two again, but, while gliding on one ski, try to make a turn by using the weighted ski's outside edge. This is not hard if you keep the weighted leg bent and push the knee forward and uphill.

4 Try to link some of these turns on the outside edges while skiing close to the fall line. Raise the unweighted ski by pulling your downhill boot up under you during the steering phase.

5 When you have mastered doing these turns close to the fall line, you should try to increase their radius. Start out by transferring your weight to the outside edge of your inside ski. While the transfer is in progress, you should push off with the ski now about to be unweighted. You will start your turn much more smoothly if you bend your legs and bank, that is, lean into the hill to counteract the centrifugal force.

(*LEFT*) Some ballet turns. (*1*) Javelin. (*2*) Flamingo. (*3*) Outrigger.
(*BELOW*) The Charleston. At the end of a short turn on the inside ski's (here, the right ski) outside edge, set the edge more. Plant your right pole. Hop to the right over your track, so that your left ski lands on its outside edge, under your right hip. Skid a little. Make a new pole plant and hop over onto the new inside ski's outside edge.

The Art Furrer (Javelin) Turn

The Art Furrer, or javelin, turn is skied on the turn's outside ski, while the inside ski is lifted up and held across the weighted ski, just in front of the binding.

Start a traverse in the natural position, weighting both skis equally. Gradually shift all your weight to the intended turn's outside ski. Lift the unweighted ski and swing it across the weighted ski, which you steer by pushing your knee into the turn. Use your outstretched arms to help you maintain balance. At the end of the turn, swing the unweighted ski back to being parallel with your other ski, put it down, and weight both skis evenly. You are now ready to make a turn in the other direction.

The Flamingo

The flamingo is a sequence of turns all done on one and the same ski, while the other ski is kept off the snow. Skiing down the fall line, you lift one ski parallel to the terrain. By bending the weighted leg

and steering with your knee, make a turn on the inside edge of the weighted ski. Then stretch the weighted leg and shift your weight to the outside edge of the ski, bend the leg again, and steer into a new turn. Plant your poles and use them to help you unweight the ski when changing edges. The flamingo can also be skied with the unweighted ski crossed over the weighted ski.

The Outrigger Turn

The outrigger turn is performed on the turn's inside ski and in a squatting position. The outside ski is practically unweighted and is extended to the side, sliding parallel to the inside ski on the snow, and the extended leg is slightly flexed. Start the turn on your inside ski by squatting and extending the unweighted outside ski to the side. At the end of the turn, lift your torso a bit and bring in the unweighted ski. You will automatically lean back in order to be able to lift and bring in the front part of the unweighted ski and turn it in the direction of the new turn. When you have established snow contact with the new inside ski, shift your weight over to it, extend the now unweighted outside leg, crouch, and start the new turn. The better your balance becomes, the less you have to lift your torso in order to shift your weight from one ski to the other. Outrigger turns can also be performed by two people holding hands while going downhill, but this requires excellent balance, good coordination, and lots of practice.

A word of warning before you start: try the outrigger position when you are stationary. If the knee of your weighted leg hurts, don't try the outrigger turn. Your knee might get damaged.

The Charleston

The Charleston is a series of rhythmically linked turns, always skied on the inside ski with the unweighted ski extended to the side, its tip still on the ground. The movements are very similar to those in the "Charleston" dance.

Practice the weight shift from one ski to the other on level terrain before you try it on a slope. Imagine that there is a line in the snow between your skis. Lift your right ski and hop on the left one across the "line," trying to land as far as possible sideways; then hop back and try to land as far as possible on the other side of the "line" on your right ski. Keep doing this, and note that the left ski swings out to make room for the right ski to land when you hop to the left, and vice versa.

The following is the sequence of movements in the Charleston. Start down the fall line in a fairly long-radius turn on your inside ski, bending your weighted leg and steering with the knee. At the end of the turn, set the edge, plant your pole close to the shovel of your weighted ski (about one-third of the ski's total length from its tip), hop smoothly in the manner described above to your previously unweighted ski, and go into your next turn. After you have practiced this for a while, try reducing the radius of your turns until you are doing rhythmic, smooth, short-radius turns down the fall line.

The Reul (Royal) Christy

The Reul christy is really named for a German skier who, in the 1930s, developed a technique based on skiing on one ski as much as possible. Today, Mr Reul's name has been distorted to Royal, and thus this turn is generally known as the royal christy.

Start by practicing the royal christy position while standing on level ground. Raise one of your skis backward—as if you were going to try and touch your neck with its tail—as you bend your upper body forward. The raised boot should preferably be level with your hips and directly behind them when you are in the middle of a turn.

When doing royal christies on a slope, you should start out with a skating step and push off with your outside ski to get all your weight on the inside ski. Bend your upper body slightly forward and rotate it in the direction of the turn while you lift the outside ski high above the snow. The tip of that ski must always be kept above the snow's surface. In this position you steer through the turn by pushing your bent knee into it, banking as you turn. Keep your hands forward and at hip level, so that your poles help you maintain balance. When the turn is almost finished, straighten your body gradually and lower the raised ski to the snow.

The Crossover

The crossover might be regarded as a combination of an uphill stepover and a royal christy. Here, too, you should start by practicing the maneuvers while standing still on level ground. Put all your weight on one ski and swing the other backward, then forward and up, until your ski tail clears the weighted ski. Cross your unweighted leg in front of your weighted leg and set down the lifted ski at a slight angle to the other ski. Then immediately stretch your body forward and shift all your weight to the previously unweighted ski, planting your poles and leaning onto them. Lift the now unweighted ski, twisting its tip away from you so that it does not get stuck in the snow, then swinging the leg to uncross it from the other. You will end up in the position you had when you started.

When you start doing the crossover while skiing, go slow in a gentle traverse in the natural position, weighting both skis evenly. Avoid using the wrist straps of your poles, and start by weighting your uphill ski. The more experience you get, the less you will have to rely on the poles when shifting your weight. Eventually, you will be able to do the crossover without using your poles at all, except as an aid to balance, and you will also be able to remain in the royal christy position long enough to carve a turn on your weighted ski.

The Tatra

The tatra is a turn which you perform on one ski with your legs crossed. Start out as if you were going to do a crossover, unweighting your outside ski and crossing it to the other side of your inside ski. Plant your pole and shift your weight to what is now your inside ski, steering by pushing your bent knee into the turn. At the end of the turn, plant your pole and shift your weight to your other ski.

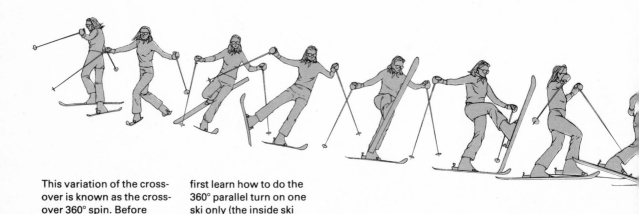

This variation of the crossover is known as the crossover 360° spin. Before attempting it, you must first learn how to do the 360° parallel turn on one ski only (the inside ski waltz).

Skiing Backward

Now that you have learned to balance on one ski when going downhill, it is time for you to learn the second fundamental step to the different ballet turns, the ability to ski backward. And, just as when you first learned to ski, the first exercise is to slide downhill with your skis in a wedge position.

Find a very gentle slope and start only a couple of yards uphill, ski tails together and ski tips spread out. Push your slightly flexed knees inward so that your skis are edged, and stand in the natural position, using your poles for support and weighting both skis evenly. Look over your shoulder to check that no one is in your way—this is something you always have to do when skiing backward. Roll your knees outward until your skis are flat on the snow, and push off with your poles to start you gliding downhill. Be careful not to bend your upper body forward; later, you should try going backward without your poles, as this will help you avoid bending over at the waist. Stop by edging your skis again at the bottom of the hill if you do not come to a stop simply because the slope ends. Go a little bit further up the hill each time you practice the backward wedge.

When you master going straight downhill in a backward wedge, you should try doing wedge turns. Traverse a gentle, mogul-free slope in a backward wedge with both skis evenly weighted and slightly edged. Keep looking over your downhill shoulder to see where you are going. To initiate the turn, shift some of your weight from your uphill to your downhill ski by bending the knee and ankle of that leg slightly. The built-in characteristics of your skis will then see to it that you turn, just as they would if you were going forward. Remember to stand on the entire soles of your feet; if you bend over forward, you will shift your weight to the balls of your feet. At the end of the turn, you will be going in a traverse again with evenly weighted skis, and you will be ready to start a new turn in the other direction. Keep doing these turns, going in steeper and steeper traverses, until you can do short-radius turns down the fall line.

The 360° Wedge Turn

To do a 360° wedge turn, start out in a traverse with your skis in the ordinary (forward) wedge position. Don't use your wrist straps; if you fall when going backward, it is better to drop the poles than to break your wrists. Weight both skis evenly and keep them slightly edged. Initiate the turn by

(LEFT) In the royal christy, your raised foot should be held level with your hips and straight behind. Take care not to catch the ski tip in the snow.

(RIGHT) Half of the 360° wedge turn is skied forward and half backward. After each half, you must end with tips higher than tails, or vice versa.

111

When skiing 360° parallel turns, you should avoid leaning too much into the center of the turn. Keep your hips directly above your boots.

ski tails and glide into another forward wedge turn, all the time anticipating it with your upper body.

Keep practicing the 360° wedge turn, gradually increasing your speed and decreasing the angle of your wedges. When you master it to such an extent that you can perform it with non-existent wedges— well, then you are doing a 360° parallel turn!

The 360° Parallel Turn (The Waltz)

The 360° parallel turn is also known as the waltz, and it is the basis of all other existing waltz turns.

Start by going down the fall line and initiate an uphill christy. Go through the turn in the usual manner but lessen the edging of your skis gradually as your tips turn uphill. Since the pressure is mainly on the shovels of your skis, this will cause your tails to skid more. When your ski tips point straight up the fall line, flatten your skis completely by moving your knees to a position directly above your skis, then shift your weight from your shovels to your tails. Turn your head in the direction of the next turn and anticipate the turn with your upper body. The rebound from your stretched muscles will then help your skis go through the new turn. End the 360° parallel turn with flattened, evenly weighted skis. Note that the turn should be practiced with the body in an upright position. Keep your hands in front of you at hip level. This turn can also be performed on one ski only and is then known as the inside ski waltz. When done on the inside ski and with the other ski balancing behind the skier in the royal christy position, the turn is known as the royal waltz.

Mogul Skiing and Aerial Acrobatics

As has already been mentioned, mogul skiing is not unlike the traditional alpine skiing, but it is commonly spiced with some jumps of the type usually classed as aerial acrobatics. The moguls are natural jumps and can make perfect launching pads for spreadeagles, back scratchers, daffies, kickouts, and helicopters (one or more 360° revolutions in the air).

The three main types of jumps used in aerial acrobatics are straight jumps, forward flips, and backward flips. While doing straight jumps, you can practice all the stunts mentioned above, and backward and forward flips can be made with or without twists.

However, if you wish to try this type of skiing, do so on a slope reserved for freestyle skiing. Remember, never jump if you cannot see where you land, never lose control, and never endanger other skiers.

weighting your downhill ski as soon as you have enough speed to be able to finish the turn with your ski tips higher uphill than your tails. As soon as you are in this position, flatten your skis and push your ski tips outward to the backward wedge position. Weight both skis evenly and look over your shoulder in the direction of the intended turn. Again, it is important that you have enough speed, this time to finish the turn with your tails further uphill than your tips. Flatten your skis as soon as the tails are in that position and end the turn by letting them glide into a parallel position. As you gain speed going forward once again, spread your

6

COMPETITIVE
ALPINE SKIING

Every accomplished skier has a yen to try his hand at competitive skiing. Admittedly, some are only interested in running a few gates for the fun of it, but there are others who are real racing enthusiasts and want to become good racers. The keen interest in alpine racing is apparent wherever some team is training round slalom poles set up on a slope. You can often see leisure skiers sneak onto the course to try it out, much to the fury of the coach or team leader! If the "sneak" competitor is good, the course will provide him with a nice challenge, but if he is bad and unable to run the gates properly, he is going to mess up the tracks between the gates and bring the full wrath of the coach down upon him.

If you want to be a good racer, you must be a good free skier. You develop a greater sense of security, better balance, and a good style—your own style—by concentrating your efforts on free skiing before starting to run the gates. High-speed skiing on free slopes will give you plenty of practice at making smooth, fast turns. Anyway, let's face it—very few leisure skiers are ever going to be top-class racers. The important thing is to become an excellent free skier in any kind of situation. Then, if you want to race, all the experience you have from the free runs will be there to back you up as you hurtle toward the gates.

In alpine skiing, there are three disciplines: slalom, giant slalom, and downhill racing. I prefer not to say that the one is harder than the other, but I have found that it is easier for people to learn to race slalom than to race giant slalom or downhill. The latter two disciplines demand very high speed, excellent timing, and good judgment (a talent for making the right turn at the right time), and it seems impossible to teach this if you do not have a feeling for it from the very start.

Slalom

According to the rules laid down by the Federation International du Ski (FIS, the organizing body for international competitive skiing), the slalom course should be composed of a certain number of gates, fifty-five to seventy-five on a vertical drop of 130—180 m (590—720 ft) for men, and forty-five to sixty on a vertical drop of 180—220 m (425—590 ft) for women. The slalom gate should consist of two solid round poles, 1.8 m (5 ft 11 inches) of which extend above the surface of the snow. The poles are almost always taped with red or blue tape and topped with flags of the same colors. Consecutive gates must always have alternating colors. The minimum width between the poles of a gate is 4 m (13 ft 1 inches), the maximum 5 m (16 ft 5 inches), and no poles may be placed closer to each other than 0.75 m (2 ft 6 inches). A slalom course should contain open and closed (blind) gates, as well as a minimum of two vertical combinations. There must also be at least four hairpin combinations, as well as combinations of open and closed gates.

In a slalom race, there are always two courses, and each is run once. The courses are set up by different course setters. The race is won by the skier who has the shortest total time for both courses. If any gate is missed, the competitor is disqualified.

As can be seen from the illustration, the gates are set in the fall line. In the starting gate, the competitor's shins strike a rod that breaks an electric circuit, thus activating an electric stopwatch. As the competitor crosses the finishing line, he breaks the photoelectric beam there and stops the stopwatch.

The first four gates are open to allow the racer to find his rhythm. They should be taken "high," which means that the turn should be started early and above the inside poles of the gates, in order to find the proper line through the gates. From the fourth gate, the skier goes into an "elbow," a combination that, in the particular course illustrated here, should be skied "under." This will give him plenty of time (relatively speaking) to turn at the sixth to go into a flush (a vertical combination). Then comes an open gate and a double hairpin, which is followed by an elbow combination, open gates, and an offset vertical combination (an offset flush). The different combinations are repeated throughout the course. The last few gates should be open and should lead the skier to the mid-point of the finishing line.

The Start

A good start is vital and can save the racer some hundredths of a second. It is almost impossible to regain time that is lost at a bad start. At the starting gate, the rod that activates the stopwatch is directly over the starting line. The racer puts his poles on the course side of the rod, so that it is his lower legs that strike it, thus activating the stopwatch, when he starts. His ski tails must not be allowed to touch anything that he might be able to use as a springboard (this is the rule in amateur racing; professional racing rules will be dealt with later). A countdown is given to the competitor, who must leave the gate within one second, plus or minus, of the "go."

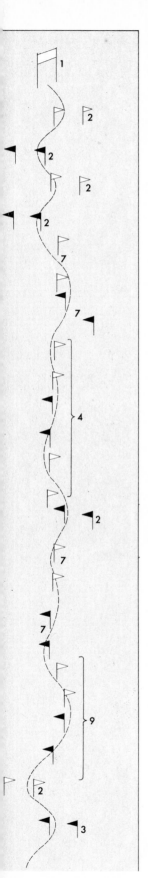
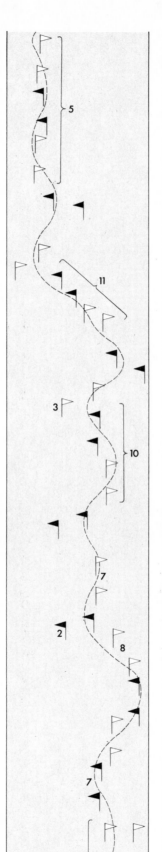
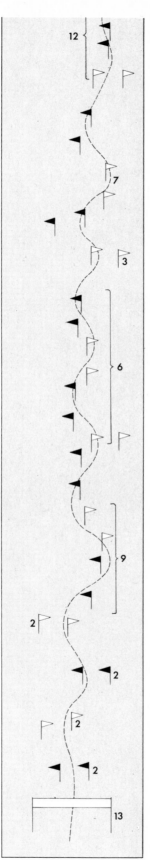

A slalom course from start to finish, with the correct line indicated. Every second gate is red and every second blue. (*1*) Start. (*2*) Open gate. (*3*) Entrance, or "elbow." (*4*) Double hairpin combination. (*5*) Vertical. (*6*) Offset flush. (*7*) Closed gate. (*8*) Half-open gate. (*9*) Broken hairpin. (*10*) Offset hairpin. (*11*) Oblique hairpin. (*12*) Seelos gate. (*13*) Finish.

The best way to start is considered to be to "drop" the upper body forward before hitting the rod with the lower legs. This movement gives an immediate impetus, so that the run will have acceleration from the very start. The gate should be built on a knoll, so that the competitor will also have this to help him pick up speed immediately. The closeness of the legs to the rod and of the rod to the poles is a matter of style and technique that varies with the individual. One important thing, though. Don't plant your poles in the deep holes that are built after a number of starts; it would be hard to get a good push-off from such holes. If the gate is not built on a knoll but on flat terrain, you should use skating steps to get to the beginning of the drop. Normally, however, the starting gate will be on a knoll and the catapult, or jump, start is the fastest.

The Catapult, or Jump, Start

This start is also known as the Killy start, as it was Jean-Claude Killy, the famous French slalom artist, who first made it known on the racing circuit. In the catapult start, the poles are planted in front of the line and the upper body is slung back. When the countdown reaches "go," the competitor puts pressure on the poles and springs forward and up (almost as a pole vaulter uses his pole). The push-off with the poles is so powerful that the skier is launched into the air. This gives him a momentum that has him moving at speed before he actually hits the rod.

It is important that, when starting, you have your skis pointed in exactly the direction in which you must go to get into a good starting-point for the first turn. Your ankles, knees, and hips will be deeply flexed, and you will have your weight on the balls of your feet, ready to spring forward. One or more powerful pushes with the poles will soon get you to racing speed.

Practice is the only way to get the timing and coordination perfect, but it is worth it, as a good start will win you valuable time.

The Finish

The advent of electronic timing equipment brought

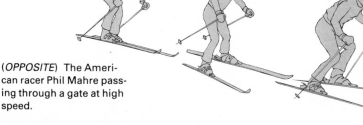

(*LEFT*) The catapult start. (*1*) The poles are planted on the course side of the rod. Ankles, knees, and hips are deeply flexed, and the racer is almost sitting, with his upper body slung back. At "go," he drives forward and upward, pushing off hard on his poles. (*2*) Some powerful pushes with his poles and, if necessary, some skating steps immediately after the start help him to increase speed.

(*BELOW*) The moment before a racer crosses the finishing line, he pushes his lower legs forward by bending sharply at the knees and bringing his rear end down fast (*1*). He thus breaks the photocell beam a fraction of a second earlier than if he had kept going in an upright position. (*2*) His stance as he crosses the finishing line.

(*OPPOSITE*) The American racer Phil Mahre passing through a gate at high speed.

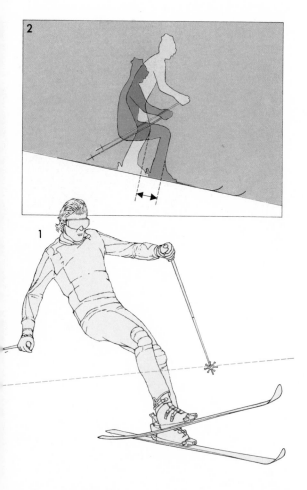

with it a lot of very bad falls, as competitors were throwing their poles, arms, and bodies forward in the effort to break the photocell beam a fraction of a second earlier. This often led to the skiers' catching their edges or falling forward quite badly. The system has now been adjusted, so that the beam will register only when broken by the skiers' legs. When this adjustment was done, a new way of finishing was developed and is still being used; the lower legs are pushed forward hard the moment before the finishing line is to be crossed. This is done by bending forward sharply at the knees while bringing the rear end down fast. If you decide to break the beam in this manner, check the height of the photocell beam before the race and make sure that you do not go too low and under the beam. Even this mode of finishing the race can be dangerous, as the competitor can end up hitting the ground with his behind, back, and hands, losing control completely.

If the finishing line is not parallel with and square before the final gate, it is more advantageous for the skier to go through the final gate from the end nearest the finishing line. Again, this should be checked before the race.

The correct stance when approaching the line from the final gate depends on whether you are tired. If not, you can make time by taking a few short skating steps. If you are tired, stay in the

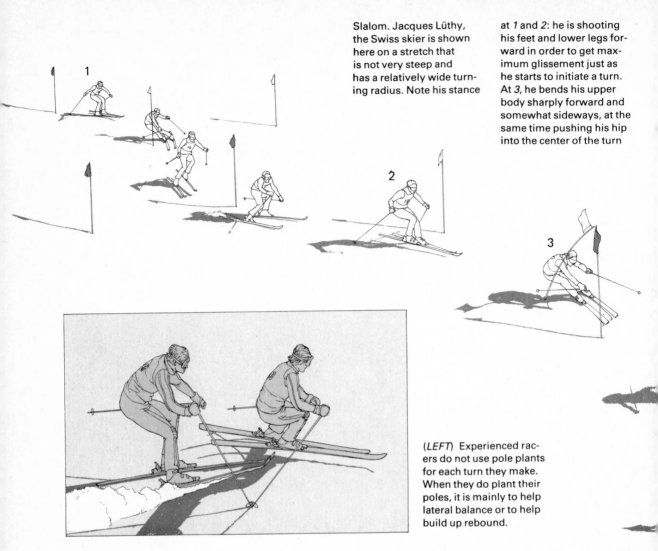

Slalom. Jacques Lüthy, the Swiss skier is shown here on a stretch that is not very steep and has a relatively wide turning radius. Note his stance at 1 and 2: he is shooting his feet and lower legs forward in order to get maximum glissement just as he starts to initiate a turn. At 3, he bends his upper body sharply forward and somewhat sideways, at the same time pushing his hip into the center of the turn

(LEFT) Experienced racers do not use pole plants for each turn they make. When they do plant their poles, it is mainly to help lateral balance or to help build up rebound.

crouched "egg" stance, as attempted skating steps can unbalance you. Another factor to consider here is, of course, the distance and the angle of the slope between the final gate and the finishing line of the course.

The Pole Plant

In racing, the pole plant is mainly used to help lateral balance. The skier keeps his arms down and forward with his poles out to support his balance. He will not plant his poles for each turn he makes, because this actually makes him lose time, as his arms become "blocked" and his shoulders and arms lock for a moment. Another use for the poles is that they help to build up rebound while the skier is jetting. If the pole plant is to help the movement, the pole must, as always, be planted forward and downhill, so that the resistance that arises—a kind of rebound—will lead to a power exchange between the poles and the skier's shoulders.

The good slalom skier needs fast-reacting knees, a "quiet" and highly coordinated upper body, and a very economical arm motion. Nowadays, the pole plant is not used to increase speed, as this is done by avoiding braking in the turns and by letting the skis run smoothly through the turns. Pushing off sideways from one ski to the other will not improve speed; it is used mainly to recover from mistakes or to find a better line for the next turn.

Speed Control

When running down a slalom course, you must always adjust the setting of your ski edges so that you can control turns and avoid braking. Sometimes, the turns demand a very aggressive and abrupt edge-set which differs from the sideslip and skid used in free skiing. Speed control must be economically done; therefore, the skis must not be directed too much across the fall line, as the time and strength lost while getting the skis back into

and stretching his inside arm forward in order to pass as close as possible to the gate's inside pole. He is not using a pole plant here, preferring to turn by stepping over onto the outside ski. In *4* and *5*, he is initiating new turns by anticipation.

(*BELOW*) A smooth method of controlling speed (*1*) is to make a push-off from a well-edged outside ski, which runs parallel to the inside ski. By pushing off from the outside ski-tail while carving the turn, you can stem your skis. (*2*) If, instead, you skid, there will be increased friction between snow and skis, and you will lose time.

the fall line are crucial. It is better to push off from a well-edged outside ski which stays parallel to the inside ski. Your tracks will then become wider; by pushing off from the outside ski-tail while carving a turn with it, you can stem your skis. The sideways push-off from the outside, or downhill, ski can be used to get a good rebound for the next turn. This smooth method of controlling speed is valuable in any combination of gates in a slalom course. Skidding instead of increasing the angle at which the skis grip will increase the friction between snow and skis and will ruin the arc of the turn.

Racing With a High Number

The main obstacles for the competitor with a high number in a slalom race are not the track-ruts in the gates but the bumps which get built up between the gates. The higher your racing number is, the greater the number of skiers who will precede you. The jet technique is helpful when negotiating the bumps already made on the slope. However, if you unweight too much, you will drop into the next rut and will not be able to start the following turn early enough, thus losing your perfect line through the gates. But if you know how to ski the ruts and how to use the centrifugal force to bank in your turns on them, you can gain speed from turn to turn.

You must reach the end of a turn in a high position and know when to begin the jetting motion before you reach the bump. Your unweighted skis, which are then pushed forward, should not lose contact with the snow and should

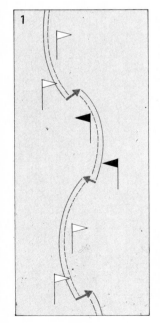
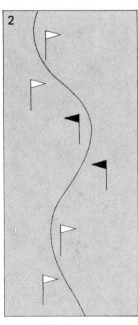

119

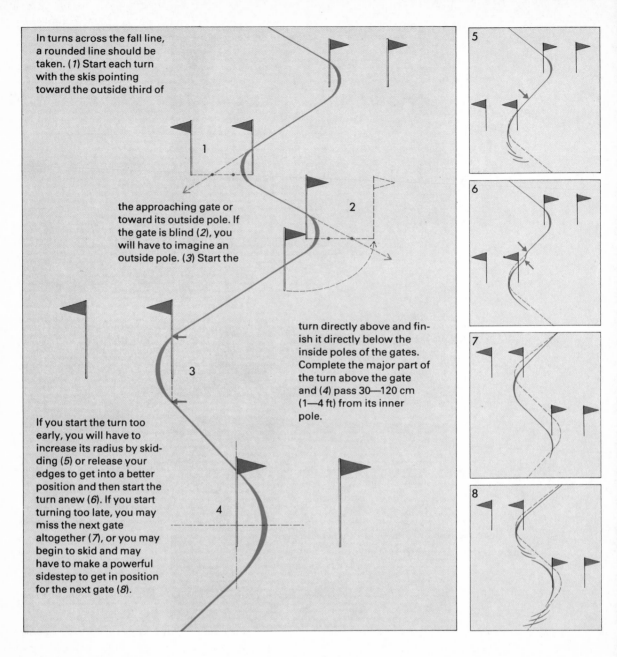

In turns across the fall line, a rounded line should be taken. (*1*) Start each turn with the skis pointing toward the outside third of

the approaching gate or toward its outside pole. If the gate is blind (*2*), you will have to imagine an outside pole. (*3*) Start the

turn directly above and finish it directly below the inside poles of the gates. Complete the major part of the turn above the gate and (*4*) pass 30—120 cm (1—4 ft) from its inner pole.

If you start the turn too early, you will have to increase its radius by skidding (*5*) or release your edges to get into a better position and then start the turn anew (*6*). If you start turning too late, you may miss the next gate altogether (*7*), or you may begin to skid and may have to make a powerful sidestep to get in position for the next gate (*8*).

immediately be steered into the coming turn. Reverse the weighting of the uphill and downhill skis to initiate the next turn.

Timing and Line

The ability to choose the correct line—that is, the path that the skis should follow—in a slalom or giant slalom course and to maintain it with precise timing is very important. Each racer must choose his own line according to his ability. The best and fastest line for one skier is not necessarily the best for another. The line a racer will take through the gates depends upon the types of turns, the rhythm of the course, the terrain, the snow condition, and his own skill.

There are two different types of turns: those across the fall line and those in the fall line. In a turn across the fall line, a rounded line should be taken. If, instead, you ski straight from gate to gate, you will cover less distance but lose time in abrupt changes of direction. Aim for a smooth, carved turn at maximum speed through each gate.

1 Start each turn with the skis pointing toward the outside pole of the upcoming gate or toward its outside third. Treat closed gates as imaginary open gates.

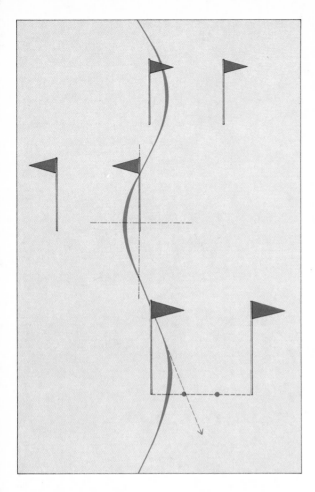

go clear of the pole and will keep you from skidding. Brushing the gate with the arm or shoulder will not affect speed or balance, but any hard contact between the pole and the front of the body should be avoided. Turns in the fall line can be skied in a straight line and at less distance to the inside pole.

Gates set in the fall line call for a different technique:

1 Start the turn with your skis pointed toward the inside pole of the upcoming gate or toward its inside third.

2 Each turn should be started directly above and finished directly below the inside pole of the upcoming gate. If the turn is started too late, you will miss the gate, whereas, if the turn is started too early, you may hook a ski tip on the inside pole and have a fall, or you may pass in front of the gate and miss it.

3 When you are skiing a course in which the gates are set close to the fall line, parallel step turns (lateral projections) can supply most of the directional changes required. By stepping from side to side, keeping the skis almost parallel, and turning them very little, you will gain time, and your skis will run a lower line at the completion of each turn and project back to a higher line for the beginning of the next turn.

Rhythm

It is often said of a competitor after he has completed an unsuccessful run that he could not "find the rhythm of the course." This may be due to a poorly planned course, but more often, the skier in question has not studied the course carefully enough to plot his tactics.

What actually can give a competitor rhythm is that the gates of a course are set in a coordinated, repeating pattern. When the gates are set across the fall line, we speak of a "round" rhythm, and if they are set in the fall line, we speak of a "straight" rhythm. In a slalom course, the rhythm will be partly round and partly straight because of the FIS rules, which require the use of several gate combinations.

The following are the fundamentals for dealing with changes in rhythm:

1 Study and memorize the course very carefully in advance, especially the key gates where the rhythm changes. Either sideslip down or walk up along the course (you are not allowed to ski it before the competition) a few times until you are sure that you remember all the different combina-

(*ABOVE*) In a course where the gates are set in the fall line, the turns should be started with the skis pointed toward the inner third of the gate or toward its inside pole. Here, too, the major part of the turn should be completed before the racer passes the gate close to the inside pole. The racer gains time by stepping sideways from inside edge to inside edge with his skis almost parallel, turning them only a very little.

2 The turn should be started directly above and finished directly below the upcoming gate. This will give you a perfect line through the course.

3 Complete the major part of the turn above the gate. Competition racers perform fifty to ninety percent of a turn above the gate and pass tightly below the inside pole to complete the turn. If most of the turn is performed below the gate, the racer will drop to an impossibly low line and will be in trouble when trying to approach the next gate.

Your skis should follow an arc which runs 30—120 cm (1—4 ft) from the inside pole, as this will allow your body—even if extremely angulated—to

tions. In every course, you will find speed traps which make the course more difficult. Sometimes—although, nowadays, it is rare—you can find combinations which you have the choice of passing in two different ways: over or under. An experienced skier should decide in advance which is best for him.

2 While running the course, you must look and think ahead. Mentally, you should always be two or three gates ahead of your skis, and the faster you go, the further you have to think ahead. Only by anticipating all changes of rhythm will you be able to react smoothly and effectively when they occur.

3 When the rhythm changes in the course, you must make sure that you ski the upcoming combinations at the proper speed and in the proper line. There are two basic types of change in rhythm: from a straight section to a round one and from a round to a straight. In the former case, you must begin to round your turns when skiing the last two gates of the straight section in order to carry as much speed as possible through the change in rhythm. If you do not "set up" for the rhythm change, you will not be able to pass the first gates of the round section without skidding or stopping to maneuver properly towards the upcoming gates.

When coming from a round section into a straight one, you should straighten your line immediately. If you continue doing rounded turns in the straight section, you will lose too much time. A quick step can help you straighten your line.

Terrain Changes

When studying a slalom course and memorizing where the changes of rhythm occur, you should also pay careful attention to the changes of terrain, as these are bound to occur at the key gates, where the rhythm changes as well. A smooth, evenly angled slope without changes of terrain simply never is used for slalom competitions.

1 When skiing from a flat section to a steep one, you should ski the first gate of the steep section in a rounded line and stay well away from the inside pole. You will then also be able to smoothly control your speed. If you ski the upcoming gate at too high a speed and in too straight a line, you will lose your rhythm and be forced to go into an abrupt turn, thereby losing time.

2 In a flat section, you should maintain—and preferably gain—as much speed as possible, even if this means you have to sacrifice some of it in the next steep section. Try to find the straightest possible line, and avoid turning and edge-setting, as this will brake your speed. Time lost on a flat

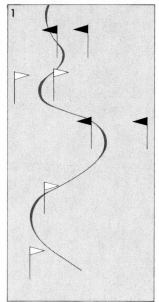
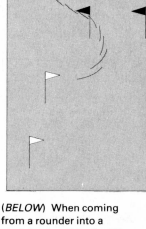

(*ABOVE*) At a change in rhythm from a straighter to a rounder section, the racer must begin to round his turns when skiing the last two gates (*1*) of the straighter section. (*2*) If the racer does not anticipate the change of rhythm, he will be forced to skid or stop to maneuver properly toward the first gate in the rounder section.

(*BELOW*) When coming from a rounder into a straighter section, the skier must immediately seek to straighten his line; a quick step (*1*) can help him do so. (*2*) The racer who continues to ski in a rounded line in the straight section will lose time.

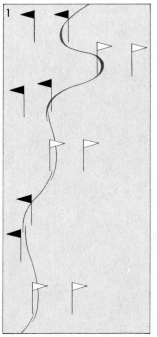
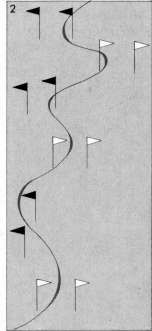

section of the course is very hard to recover, so maximum speed is vital there.

3 Moguls and deep ruts which have been built up by competitors running before you may affect your choice of line. To be able to pass such obstacles successfully, you may have to finish turns before moguls, turn round moguls, or bank your turns on ruts.

Snow Conditions

Snow conditions vary from race to race and are extremely important to the competitors, as the condition of the snow decides what kinds of turn can be made and at which speed they can be performed. If the snow is firm, so that your ski edges get a good grip, you can make tight turns. If the course is icy, use more rounded turns to allow your ski edges to hold their bite, but you must be careful not to skid, as you may then miss the next gate. Hard, abrupt turns on soft snow will cause you to lose speed; under those conditions, a rounded, soft line is recommended.

Timing

Proper timing means that body and ski movements are coordinated so that a desired line can be followed. The optimal result of timing is that a single turn of consistent radius is made at each gate, and that the turn is started in the correct place, which is equivalent to its being started at the correct time. Every turn should be initiated directly above the inside pole of the upcoming gate as soon as your skis begin to move in a new direction after an edge change. The turn as such will not occur until you have made the coordinated body movements known as the "initiation phase" of a turn—up-unweighting, down-unweighting, lateral projection, anticipation, and pole plant. For proper timing, it is important that you are aware of these movements and know how to use them. Your timing will also be affected by your ability to initiate a turn, by the speed you maintain throughout the turn, and by your movement alertness. The only way in which you can discover the exact point where you need to initiate a turn is by doing a lot of practice running the gates, as the point will vary with the individual skier's skill and approach.

Technique and Tactics

Individual skiers will develop their own styles, but all skiing is mainly a combination of two factors: technique and tactics. Every error a skier makes can thus be classified as either technical or tactical, or both, one leading to the other.

So what is technique and what is tactics? The following will help you distinguish between the two.

Technique

1 The basic performance of the various turns.
2 The automatic, correct movement of the skis in any situation.
3 Free skiing—the skier's personal style.
4 The skier's use of his body: is he in a natural, relaxed position? How does he make use of his feet, lower and upper legs, hips, upper body? What is his arm and hand discipline like—any unnecessary moves? What is his balance like?
5 Body stance throughout the turns.
6 Edge set and angulation of knees and hips in slow-speed and high-speed turns.
7 Body stance while turning in different kinds of terrain.

Tactics

1 The timing of turns—long-radius, medium-radius, short-radius.
2 Rhythm changes.
3 Changes of technique because of changes in the terrain or because of the condition of the snow.
4 Preparations before the start: warming-up and concentration exercises. Careful inspection of the course. Careful preparation of equipment—waxing, filing, etc.

A good way to learn how to recognize mistakes and overcome them is to study your own style as well as that of other skiers on films or video tapes. Run the films both at normal speed and in slow-motion, and look closely for any mistakes.

Technical Mistakes

1 Leaning into a turn on a hill.
2 Over-rotating.
3 Leaning too far back or forward.
4 Jack-knifing of the upper body.
5 Lack of angulation (moving hips sideways toward the center of the turn).
6 Hip rotation.
7 Unnecessary movements of hands, arms, upper body, and head.

Tactical Mistakes

1 Timing errors—performing the initiation or the finishing phases of a turn too early or too late.

2 Use of the wrong technique with regard to the snow and course conditions.

3 Careless or incomplete preparations.

Slalom Training

Slalom training should be continued throughout the year. During the summer months, you can practice running through forests, making turns round trees, or you can set up poles on a field and maneuver your way round them as fast as you can run, thus simulating the multi-directional changes in a slalom course. Summer skiing on snow is also possible at high altitudes, where you will find either ice or firn snow. All summer skiing should be concentrated and continuous; preferably, it should be done for several hours a day for at least a week. At this time of the year, however, it is advisable to practice at a more moderate speed than usual, so that you will be able to recognize your mistakes and correct them. Concentrate on training your technique and on "breaking in" new equipment.

Success Tactics

Study the course until you know it by heart. Find out where the difficulties occur, where there are changes of rhythm, terrain, and snow conditions, as well as where the easier parts are, for in those, you should be able to gain some time. Watch the competitors who run before it is your own turn. It is important to see how they handle the terrain and

the various snow conditions. Setting up too early or too late for a turn, edging too much or too little, skidding in the turns, and initiating the same turn twice are all mistakes which will be made by those who have not memorized the course properly. Concentration is all-important. Still, don't be so eager to watch your competitors that you miss your own start! Also, remember that, if you have a high starting number, the course will become cut up and badly worn, so suit your tactics to the course.

The second run in a slalom competition is often a problem for all the remaining competitors. Those who managed a good first run will be nervous that their second will not be as good, and those who made a bad first run will worry about the prospect of making an even worse second run. A good general rule is this: if you are among the ten best in the first run, you should start the second more carefully than if you are further down the list, in which case you have nothing to lose and might as well give all you have to give. Since the time difference between the winner's run and that of the competitor who ends up in the twentieth place may be as little as a second, you still have a chance in the competition even if you happen to have ended up pretty far down the list in the first run. Who knows—maybe it is your day for making a perfect second run, with all the fantastic coordination of tactics and technique you've dreamt of!

(*LEFT*) An outstanding technical racer—Sweden's Ingemar Stenmark, double world champion at Garmisch-Partenkirchen in 1978 and gold medalist in both slalom and giant slalom at the 1980 Olympic Games at Lake Placid.

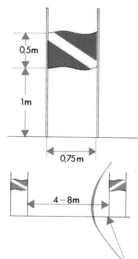

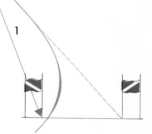

(*LEFT*) The measurements of a giant slalom gate according to the FIS rules. The distance (*1*) between the inner poles of two consecutive gates must exceed 10 m (33 ft), and the vertical drop between the two gates should be 8 m (26 ft).

0,5m

1m

0,75m

4 – 8m

1

Giant Slalom

Like slalom competitions, all giant slalom events consist of two runs, and the race is won by the competitor who has the best total time for both courses. According to the FIS rules, the vertical drop for the women's courses should be 250—350 m (820—1,150 ft) and that for the men's should be 250—400 m (820—1,312 ft). In World Cup races the vertical drop for both the women's and the men's courses must exceed 300 m (984 ft).

The number of gates in a giant slalom course should be fifteen percent of its vertical drop in meters plus or minus three gates. Thus, a vertical drop of 400 m would mean fifty-seven to sixty-three gates.

A giant slalom gate consists of two pairs of poles which are taped in red or blue. A red or blue flag, measuring 0.5×0.75 m (20×30 inches) and having a white, diagonal stripe is held tightly between each pair of poles. The diagonal stripe must point in the direction of descent, and the bottom edge of each flag should be 1 m (3 ft 3 inches) above the surface of the snow.

The FIS rules further indicate that the course should be at least 30 m (98 ft) wide. The vertical drop between the gates should be 8 m (26 ft), and the gates should be 4—8 m (13—26 ft) wide. The distance between the inside poles of two consecutive gates must be at least 10 m (33 ft). The starting gate should be 0.75 m (30 inches) wide, and the finishing line must be at least 10 m (33 ft) wide for safe passage. The flags of closed, or blind, gates must be rolled up to a distance of 0.3 m (12 inches), so that they do not obstruct the racer's view.

The courses used for both runs in a giant slalom competition will be set up the day before the race. Most combinations used in giant slalom courses are open and closed gates, but sometimes, combinations like elbows and hairpins are also used by the course-setter. During the day of the race, the courses will remain closed to training, but the competitors are allowed to study them by climbing up along the courses on skis or to sideslip down their sides. Just as in slalom, any competitor who skis through the gates in advance will be disqualified. While studying the courses, every racer must wear his bib-number visibly. However, the slopes that are used for the competition must be open for training some days before the courses are set up.

In a giant slalom course, the gates are set further apart than in a slalom course, and the racer's speed will thus be higher. Further, the giant slalom course is much longer and covers more difficult terrain. The racer's time in a run must exceed sixty seconds.

How to Ski a GS Course

When interviewed after a giant slalom race, one competitor may say that he found himself putting too much pressure on the edges; another may complain that he could not find a proper line and started his turns too late in several gates. A third

might suggest that he lost the race through skidding in one gate, and many will say that they overturned, that is, they kept too much pressure on the outside ski for too long.

Giant slalom really could be described as a series of traverses across the fall line. Speed is mainly built up during the traverses, and it takes a good skier to use exactly the right amount of edging in them. Timing and coordination in the turns have to be right as well, and the skier who finds the

When approaching a gate set close to the fall line, you can gain time by skiing in an even steeper traverse (1), closer to the fall line, and then step laterally (2) to get into a good position for the approaching turn. Try to carve the turn (3), and pass close to the inside pole in a wide stance and—preferably— with parallel skis.

straightest line through the gates and makes the fewest mistakes will always win.

The most commonly used turn in giant slalom is the step turn. When approaching a gate in a traverse which is close to the fall line, time may be gained by skiing closer to the fall line and then stepping laterally to get into a good position for the turn. If you stay too far away from the inside pole of a gate, your turn will be smooth, but you will lose time. Turns should be carved; the more snow you spray when turning, the more you are skidding

rather than carving. Try to keep your skis parallel in a wide stance. You will rarely push your skis into a wedge position to edge them, since your speed would then make them skid, and all skidding means loss of time.

Edge your skis just before the fall line after having turned them slightly in the desired direction. Make sure that the edges bite throughout the turn. If you edge your skis too early, you will get a long-radius turn and miss the upcoming gate. Exactly when you should start a turn is determined by the desired radius of the turn, the terrain, your speed, and your ability to carve a turn properly, but generally, it is wise to start turning when your ski tips have passed an imaginary, vertical line from the inside pole of the approaching gate. At this point, pressure should be applied so that the skis go into reverse camber and bite all along their edges.

The lateral step used to get into a good line when approaching a gate may be either a skating step or a scissor step. These steps may seem very similar but differ quite a lot from each other. A skating step should be a forceful, accelerating push-off from the downhill leg and is used before long-radius turns where time allows. A scissor step is rather a glide to the uphill leg while glissement is maintained. ("Glissement" means maximum glide, that is, the glide you get when the ski is edged as little as possible without going into a sideslip.)

The best way to find out exactly where you should begin your turns, and to get familiar with the skating and scissor steps, is to run as many gates as you possibly can.

Giant Slalom Training

It is usually even more difficult to get giant slalom practice than to get slalom practice. For one thing, as the gates are wider and set further apart and the course is longer, a giant slalom course takes up too much space for the liking of other skiers in a popular skiing area. Another reason is that the course must be changed after a number of runs so that deep ruts do not get built up. Mostly, giant slalom practice can thus take place only four days a week, so that all the slopes are open to public skiing during weekends.

An adequately steep course of 300—500 m (984—1,640 ft) will be excellent for giant slalom practice. Double poles should be used for the insides of the gates, whereas the outsides can consist of single poles, as this will suffice to give the training racer an idea of the direction in which he should point his skis while finishing one turn and beginning another. With single poles only on

3

both sides of the gates, it will be difficult to set up different giant slalom combinations even for practice. Start your giant slalom practice with easy gate combinations, so that you learn how much speed you can carry through a turn.

Start and finish in a giant slalom course are skied in the same way as in a slalom course (see p. 117).

Tactics

Before the race, while memorizing the course, you should pay extra attention to the terrain, since you will be going through the gates at a much higher speed than in slalom. Nowadays, you are no longer allowed to ski parallel to the ideal line and close to the outside poles of the gates while inspecting the course. A tough jury will immediately disqualify you if you are caught skiing through even one gate before the race.

Since a giant slalom course is very long—it will take you more than sixty seconds to run—the wise competitor saves some of his energy for the last part of the course. Many racers lose by overtaxing themselves during the first two-thirds of the course, then making mistakes from being too tired.

After the first run, the course will be re-set for the second run (or both first and second runs will have been set up the previous day). If you have ended up as one of the top ten of the first run, you should ski the second one more carefully than if you end up further down the list, just as in slalom. Since the runs in giant slalom are so much longer, however, the difference in time between the best racer's run and that of no. 20 is likely to be bigger than in slalom. Remember to watch carefully the competitors who run before you, to see how they deal with the different gates.

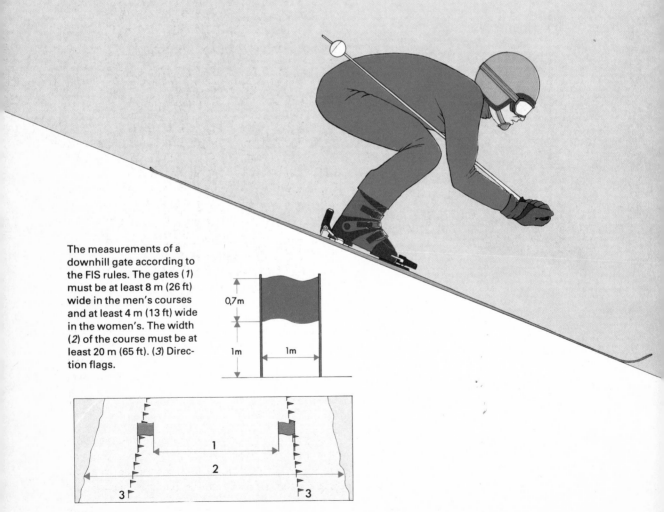

The measurements of a downhill gate according to the FIS rules. The gates (1) must be at least 8 m (26 ft) wide in the men's courses and at least 4 m (13 ft) wide in the women's. The width (2) of the course must be at least 20 m (65 ft). (3) Direction flags.

0,7 m

1m

1m

1

2

3

3

The only way to become a successful giant slalom racer is to practice, practice, and practice again. Enter as many competitions as you possibly can, and remember that good preparation—both physical and mental—before the races is vital.

Downhill Racing

Safe downhill courses are getting increasingly difficult to set up, since it is important that they are as free as possible from bumps and ruts. This means that other skiers must not ski in the course or cross it, and with the immense growth of the number of skiers in any given skiing area during recent years, this is becoming well-nigh impossible to attain. Further, the better (=faster) the skis are getting, the wider the courses have to be, since the downhill racers must have enough room for a bad fall. A

A racer in the "egg" position, here seen from the side (*LEFT*) and front (*ABOVE*). Since the racer practically forces down his upper body between his thighs and stretches his arms forward, the air drag is the least possible.

further safety measure, that of keeping the courses as smooth as possible to lessen the risk of falling, has also contributed to increasing the speed at which the racers can go. Good snow conditions are a must.

The skis used for downhill skiing are much longer than those used for slalom and giant slalom and will be 215—225 cm (7—7 ft 4 inches) long. The longer the skis, the better the skier's stability, especially in the turns. The skis must also have enough flex to absorb shocks from little bumps in the terrain without beginning to chatter. The special poles are also longer than those used for the other alpine disciplines; further, they are bent, so that they can be held close to the thighs, and the baskets have a different design. Goggles are, of course, necessary, as they are for all types of alpine skiing, and a well-fitting crash helmet must be worn.

According to the FIS rules, a downhill course must be a minimum of 20 m (65 ft) wide—30 m (98 ft) or more at dangerous spots—from tree line to tree line. The width of the gates must be at least 8 m (26 ft), that of the starting gate must be 0.75 m (30 inches), and that of the finishing line 15 m (49 ft). The color of the gates is red for men's courses and blue for the women's, if the same slope is used for both. If not, blue gates will be used. The size of the flags is 1×0.7 m (39×28 inches), and there should be a clearance of 1 m (39 inches) from the surface of the snow to the bottom edge of the flags. Direction flags on the left side of the course are red; on the right, green. If visibility is bad, additional markers—small pine branches—are used to mark both edges of the course. In the World Cup and the Olympics, the men's downhill course must take more than 120 seconds to run and the women's must take more than 100 seconds. The vertical drop should be 800—1,000 m (2,624—3,280 ft) for men's courses and 500—700 m (1,640—2,296 ft) for women's.

Great demands are made on a good downhill racer. His skiing technique as well as his physical fitness must be perfect, he must be very agile, have great endurance, and be able to concentrate continuously during the race. Further, he needs a lot of courage. The course must be laid out so that it tests the racer on all these points, which means that it will contain a concentration of technical difficulties.

The general characteristics of a downhill race are that it must be possible to ski it from start to finish without using poles and that the terrain must be cleared of all stumps, stones, and suchlike, so that the racer does not risk hitting such obstacles, even if snow is scarce on the course. The speed of the racers must be kept within reasonable limits. This is achieved with control gates, which limit the average speed and are also used to guide the competitors past tricky or dangerous points. There must be no hard, sharp ridges on the course, and all bumps must be leveled. No steep ledges should be included, as they would cause the competitors to become airborne for long distances. Convex, outward curves are not allowed, and the course must become wider where the racers' speed will increase. On the outside of curves which will be taken at great speed, there must be plenty of obstacle-free space, so that a competitor who falls and goes off the course will not collide with a tree or suchlike. Obstacles which the competitors might hit if running off the course must be thickly covered with straw bales or snow, or be protected by safety nets.

The Straight Downhill Run

All the basics of the straight run, which are discussed in chapter three, are used in downhill racing. An open stance will give you more stability, and your balance will be better if you keep your ankles, knees, hips, and upper body slightly flexed forward. Keep your muscles loose, and stand on the whole foot whenever you can to make a perfect glide possible. Always look ahead to anticipate changes of terrain. Your ability to adjust smoothly to any changes will determine the speed at which you can pass them.

As you probably know, Newton's first law states that an object will remain where it is, or will move at uniform speed in the same direction, until it is acted upon by an outside force. The forces which act upon a skier are gravity, the friction of his skis against the snow, and the air drag. Thus, when these forces are constant, the skier's speed will be constant. The steeper the hill is, the less the resistance against the gravitational force pulling the skier down the hill will be, and the faster he will go. To attain the least possible air drag and thus increase his speed even further, a downhill racer will frequently crouch to the so-called egg position. It is also important that he wears a tight racing suit; however, it is highly unlikely that the surface finish of the material should have any influence on the air resistance. In certain sections of a downhill course, the speed of the competitors will frequently exceed 100 km/h (62 mph).

To decide the rate of the skier's acceleration when he starts from rest on a slope, Newton's

(*ABOVE*) When confronted with a big bump, the downhill racer retracts his legs and stretches his hands down in front of him at the same time, to avoid being thrown up into the air by the bump. This makes him look as if he were leaning back, which is not the case.

(*BELOW*) As soon as the racer passes the crest of the bump, he stretches his legs forward and down to regain quickly his contact with the snow and to be able to make a soft landing by flexing his legs.

second law can be applied. It states that any change of movement—speed as well as direction—of a body will be proportional to the acting force, which equals the product of the mass and the change of speed. Thus, the rate of increase of the skier's speed is directly proportional to the resistance to the force of gravity, that is, the steepness of the slope. By means of what is known as dynamic forces, the skier can accelerate or retard his speed. The more abruptly a skier changes his speed and/or direction, the greater the forces involved will be,

for, as Newton's third law states, for every action, there will be an equal and opposite reaction. The effects of weighting and unweighting skis will thus be greater the more energetically these movements are performed. Similarly, the forces acting on the skier and his skis during a dynamic turning maneuver are directly proportional to the skier's speed at any given moment, and they will increase if the radius of the turn is decreased. In Newton's third law, you also find a good reason for avoiding all unnecessary body movements.

The speed limit in downhill racing sets in at the point where air resistance makes further acceleration impossible. In certain sections of the course, it will also be necessary for the racer to straighten up from his crouched position in order to be able to maneuver. This will, of course, increase the air resistance; thus, the racer who is able to stay the longest in the egg position during a race is likely to end up with the best time.

How to Ski a Downhill Race

The most important thing in a downhill race is to keep the skis as flat as possible on the ground to get the best gliding effect. On easy sections, you should ski loosely; your skis will then adjust themselves to changes in the terrain, and you will be able to roll your knees smoothly in and out as the

changes occur. Don't lean too far back or forward from the downhill position, as this will make you tighten your joints and slow down. The distance you keep between your skis is also important. If you keep them too far apart, they will pick up a lot of perpendicular rebound and you will lose your balance. Skis which are held too close to each other will also pick up rebound, which has to be absorbed. In the best tracking position, you will get a minimum of these types of shock and will be able to keep your skis flat on the snow. Your body position should be very low; preferably, your back should be parallel to the ground. The wider your tracks become, the lower down you can hold your upper body. Keep your lower legs perpendicular to your skis. (Downhill ski boots are less angled forward than ordinary slalom boots.)

Absorbing Shocks from Bumps

Today, special machinery is used in many ski areas for trail preparation. During the summer, bumps and abrupt changes of terrain are smoothed out, and in winter, the snow is packed down and bumps which are built up by the skiers are cut down. Modern downhill trails thus look like very wide, smooth roads running down the slopes. Such trails make for high speeds, but the challenge of dealing with bumps is more or less lost.

However, if you are confronted with bumps in a downhill race, it is important to remember not to lean too much forward or back. Pre-jumping used to be the most common way to maneuver on bumps in downhill races. The racer starts his jump shortly before reaching the crest of a bump to avoid the trampoline effect a jump from the crest would cause. He will then land just past the bump instead of being airborne for a longer distance, which would make him lose speed.

The modern technique used to maneuver on bumps makes the racer look as if he were leaning back, although he is not. Instead, he retracts his legs, which has a jack-knifing effect on his body and enables him to lift his skis in front of him, thus absorbing the shocks with his legs without moving his upper body vertically. With this technique, the braking effect will be kept to a minimum. When you land after this type of maneuver, you should stretch your legs slightly. Your upper body will then automatically move forward and you will end up in good balance. Further, when you retract your legs, you also do some balancing out by leaning your upper body forward. Practice this way of

The best way to initiate a turn at high speed and in a crouched position is to push the outside knee into the turn. When the outside ski is edged, it will begin to turn in the desired direction because of its side-cut.

dealing with bumps to get the "feel" of how much your skis will lift. Just before the crest of a bump, you should assume a very low position: thighs close to chest, arms forward and to the side. You will appear to be leaning back, but you will be in balance. After the crest of the bump, stretch your legs forward and down in a jetting motion to keep contact with the snow or to renew contact with it as soon as possible. If your speed is very high, you may jump farther than planned and should then remain in the crouched position slightly longer before stretching to land smoothly. Actually, birds landing on water stretch their legs in much the same way.

During downhill turns in the upright position, the racer is supported on his outside ski from the very start. Perfect hip angulation is necessary for him to be able to carry his weight directly over his outside ski's inside edge. The inside ski is then lifted completely off the snow during the rest of the turn.

Turning in a Downhill Race

The high speeds attained by the competitors in a downhill race require turning techniques different from those used in slalom or giant slalom. Most turns are performed in a crouched position, and the best way to initiate such a turn is to push your outside knee into the turn. The outside ski will then be edged and, because of its sidecut and waist, it will turn in the desired direction. Centrifugal force will then make you weight your outside ski more than your inside ski, which will remain more or less flat on the snow throughout the turn. This type of turn is actually very easy to learn and is useful in the easier sections of the course, since it can be performed at high speed. It can also sometimes be used in more difficult terrain and for medium-radius turns, as well as in banked sections. If the turn is performed when the skier is in a more upright position, he must angulate his hips more.

Many turns are also skied in a very upright position; most Austrian skiers still favor this and have done so for a long time. The technique of the upright turn, too, is very simple. The initiation is an almost imperceptible hopping motion, and the inside ski is lifted off the snow during the turn. The secret lies in the support on the outside ski from the beginning of the turn onward. At high speeds, you must weight your skis equally and have a good stance, keeping your center of gravity between your boots and your skis free to react from tip to tail. In this turn, your weight should be carried directly over your downhill ski, and this will require perfect hip angulation. Your outside ski and leg must do all the work in the turn, and you must keep stretching and bending that leg to effectively absorb shocks caused by bumps in the terrain. Further, the leg must be locked sideways so that you can keep the line of the turn, and your hip angulation requires that you keep your arms down and to the side for balance. This turn can be compared to a turn carved with the ski tail; in such a turn, however, you need to weight your heels slightly.

Slowing Down

The downhill racer can brake his speed by simply rising from a crouched to an upright position. The air resistance will then increase, and you may lose up to twenty percent of your speed. In order to keep your balance, you must rise slowly and keep your arms to your sides.

Another way of braking is to use braquage, that is, to twist your skis until they are perpendicular to the direction you are running in. However, this can be a dangerous maneuver if you are at very high speed, as you may well find yourself off the track instead of skidding down it as intended. Also, before you use braquage in the finishing area of the race, make sure that there is enough room for you to come to a halt before you run into the audience.

When the trail is going across a slope, braking is easy. Just sideslip and weight your tails. On a wide track, you can stem your skis to slow down easily and safely.

As one competitor after the other runs the downhill course, the ideal line will become bumpy in turns where everyone edges his skis sharply, and ruts will build up. If you have to go slower across these sections, you should brake your speed before you enter them; otherwise, you will use up too much of your energy and strength trying to slow down while turning. However, if you have already entered a turn and feel yourself going too fast, you should put your outside ski slightly across the slope to brake, letting your inside ski keep the track so that you will be ready to set up for the next turn.

Training

There are few areas where you can really train downhill racing. A racing course usually consists of combinations of long, straight runs and traverses, both easy and difficult ones, wide- and medium-radius turns, serpentine turns, and drop-offs. It is hard to match these conditions in training, and because of the ever-increasing number of other skiers, downhill runs which are really long enough are rare. Often, they are too easy or too difficult, and many are too narrow, making them dangerous to run at high speed. You will often have to concentrate your training to the very early morning and late afternoon hours, when few other skiers are out and snow conditions generally are very bad. Despite this, you should try to get as experienced as you possibly can, for if you train on slopes where the snow is in poor condition, you will have to concentrate immensely on what you are doing. As a contrast, the well-prepared racing course may then well seem to be almost easy.

Tactics

A downhill course will be 2,500—3,000 m (8,200—9,840 ft) long and will, as has been mentioned, take at least 100 (women) or 120 (men) seconds to run.

Before running the course in a race, the prospective competitors will have to complete successfully at least two timed training runs on it. Generally, a trail map is handed out to each racer when he signs up for his bib number. From studying this map, you will get a general idea of what the course is like. Map in hand, you should then go to the slope and check out spots where you can stop after trying out section by section of the course for the best line downhill. Don't ski the sections at racing speed, and use an upright position, so that you can oversee the run. Stop at the end of each section and consider whether you can find a better line than the one you just skied. Note especially all changes in the terrain; a mogul may mean an upcoming jump, for instance. Memorize the sections in order from start to finish. During the next course inspections you should make fewer and fewer stops until you are able to run the course non-stop. In this way, you will really get to know the difficult spots and how to remedy the initial mistakes you made at them. If you have the opportunity, ski down the course together with a coach who can advise you.

The day before the race, there will be non-stop runs which you should ski at high speed to find out your limits. Keep your eyes open before and after your own runs to study how your competitors are doing. Make absolutely sure that you have memorized the whole course and know your line throughout it. Just before the race, information on any changes of the course or the snow conditions will generally be transmitted to the competitors by radio from coaches and trainers standing along the course, but if this is not the case, you will have to check the whole course yourself. Service personnel will double-check your safety bindings before you start and will also usually help you re-wax your skis, if necessary. Remember to warm up properly before the race, and don't hang around the starting gate waiting for your turn. You will only get cold and, besides, you might well be in the way.

Parallel Events

In parallel slalom, two (or more) racers run simultaneously down two (or more) courses, which are set up side by side. The courses must be as identical as possible, including the condition of the snow, and both must be set up by the same course-setter. The vertical drop should be 80—100 m (260—330 ft), and each course will have 20—30 gates plus the starting and finishing gates and should take 20—25 seconds to run. In amateur racing, artificial jumps are not permitted.

Each course is set with a series of gates, poles, or single gates. The single gates consist of two poles with a 0.3×0.7 m (12×28 inches) flag held tightly between them. The lower edge of the flag should be 1 m (3 ft 3 inches) above the surface of the snow, so that it is impossible for the racers to duck under them. When only two courses are used, the poles and banners are red on the course to the left, as seen from the start, and blue on the course to the right. The horizontal distance between the two courses, from inside pole to inside pole of two parallel gates, as well as the distance from inside pole to inside pole of two consecutive gates in the courses, must be no less than 6 m (19 ft 8 inches) and no more than 7 m (23 ft), and that is also the distance between the starting gates. The first gate in each course should be placed no less than 6 m (19 ft 8 inches) and no more than 10 m (33 ft) from the starting gate. The finishing gates must be 7 m (23 ft) wide and be parallel to the starting gates. Each finishing gate is marked by two flags.

The racers are usually started by a sound system, and a clock shows the last five seconds so that both (all) racers start simultaneously. The entire runs are not timed; instead, the first competitor who crosses his finishing line and breaks the photoelectric beam there will start a chronometer and receive the time "zero." The following racer or racers will be timed from then on until they, too, break the photoelectric beams in their finishing gates. Often, the finish is also registered by an automatic printout. Each match between two racers consists of two runs, and the racers change courses for the second run. The contest is open to a maximum of thirty-two racers, sixteen of whom will go to the finals. Usually, the top thirty-two racers in the FIS point list of slalom and giant slalom racers will compete.

In the first qualification run, racer no. 1 on the point list will compete against racer no. 32 in group 1; racer no. 2 on the point list will compete against racer no. 31 in group 2; racer no. 3 on the point list will compete against racer no. 30 in group 3; and so on. The winner of each group is, of course, the one who has the lowest total time for his two runs.

In the second elimination run, the winner of group 8 races the winner of group 9; the winner of group 7 races the winner of group 10; the winner of group 6 races the winner of group 11; and so on. The remaining eight winners will go on to the quarter finals, in which the winner of the 1st/16th group races the winner of the 8th/9th; the winner

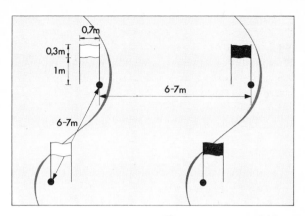

The measurements laid down by the FIS for two parallel gates and two consecutive gates in parallel slalom courses.

of the 2nd/15th group races the winner of the 7th/10th; and so on.

The losers of the quarter finals will then race each other for the 5th, 6th, 7th, and 8th position, whereupon the semifinals will take place. The losers of the semifinals then race each other for the 3rd and 4th place, and the two winners will finally compete for the 1st and 2nd place. Just as in other big alpine skiing events, the racers will be awarded FIS points according to where on the prize list they ended up.

Parallel events are also included in World Pro Skiing, where competitors race for money as well as for FIS points. In professional slalom and giant slalom competitions, two or three artificial jumps are built into the courses, and this makes the races more difficult.

The rules for professional parallel events differ slightly from those for the amateur events. The pro tour consists of about a hundred racers, the best twenty of whom are directly qualified to compete among the thirty-two who will partake in the contest. The remaining eighty-odd racers have to qualify in the so-called Friday Cup, which takes place on

Two skiers battling against
each other on the parallel
slalom course.

Friday mornings. The best three racers set the time—the entire races are timed—and the other skiers will have to match this time, give or take five percent, to qualify. The twelve best racers will be allowed to enter the first elimination run together with the twenty racers who are automatically qualified. This run takes place on Friday afternoon, and those who manage the eight best times in the blue and red courses respectively will go on to the second elimination run. Each competitor is allowed two runs, and the courses will include artificial jumps. During the following days, finals will be skied in both slalom and giant slalom. The fastest racer in the blue course will compete against the slowest racer in the red course; the second fastest racer in the blue course will compete against the second slowest racer in the red course; and so on. If a racer falls or skis across an imaginary line between the two courses in his first race, he will be disqualified and will race with a time disadvantage

of 1.5 seconds in the second race—and that disadvantage means that he has to win by at least one and a half gate, which is very difficult to accomplish.

In professional races, the starting gates differ from those used in amateur racing. The starter counts: "Ten seconds, racers ... ready ... set ... go!" and pushes a button, which causes a signal to sound and the doors in the gates to open. In the starting gate the racers can push off from a board under their ski tails, which gives them extra speed. The technique in professional skiing does not differ much from that used in amateur slalom or giant slalom races, but the artificial jumps in the professionals' courses make the contests extra exciting. In the finals a competitor will have to win eight runs to be the final victor. All the sixteen competitors who make it to the finals will win sums of money, and the first prize is several thousand dollars.

7

THE SKI
RESORT

What is the perfect ski resort, the perfect winter vacation site? Is there such a place, or is the judgment merely relative, being a reflection of your personal situation (family, newly-wed, single), your budget (spartan, generous, unlimited), your skills (beginner, intermediate, advanced), the weather patterns, the season (they are reversed, remember, on opposite halves of the Equator), the accessibility, the food, and a myriad amenities other than skiing? Ponder the matter with even the least bit of objectivity and obviously, you will find that perfection is relative. The perfect resort is a matter of "to each his own."

"Isn't this perfect!" The remark was a flat declaration of fact and in no way a question. "I'm ten minutes by car from home. These three chair-lifts operate from very early in the morning to almost midnight. There are no crowds in the off hours. The runs are barely a mile long, less than expert—in fact, after three days of skiing, anyone could handle them all—and they are very well groomed at all times. I love to go fast and feel the wind in my face."

The speaker is a man who has traveled widely. This was his second season of skiing. His skis were just over 1 m (3 ft 4 inches) in length. He is a retired physician living not far from Boston. The place he is speaking of is a small local resort, a way-station really. No overnight accommodation is provided at the slope site itself, though many commercial motels exist along the nearby highway, more for use by itinerant businessmen than for skiers. Yet the doctor has found, almost in his backyard, his perfect winter skiing retreat.

"If there's anyplace in the world better'n this, it sure doesn't have to be." This time the speaker is a 12-year-old—the son of a local cowboy—riding one of the thirty-five lifts that provide up to 1,000 m (3,280 ft) of vertical descent at Aspen, Colorado. He does not realize the import of this words, untraveled as he is. Yet he is speaking about one of the few places in North America which can be categorized as an international-class, full-service ski resort. Aspen is great, but is it perfect? And if so, for whom?

"After ten years of skiing Europe's best during winter vacations—including the new super resort complexes in France—I now go exclusively to the Canadian Rockies for helicopter skiing—to the Bugaboos, the Cariboos, the Monashees." The speaker this time is a middle-aged investment broker from New York's Wall Street, obviously well-to-do and necessarily an expert skier. Helicopter skiing, exclusive of room and board, can run in excess of U.S. $250 (c. £125) per day. Snow conditions range from ideal, waist-deep powder to very difficult, breakable crusts.

Were one to query a socialite skier, undoubtedly the idea of perfection would be Gstaad, St. Moritz, Megève, or Vail, or another of some half-dozen additional places considered to be *très chic* for the *très riches*—not that such resorts do not also offer superior skiing.

And what of the single skier? The opportunity to meet members of the opposite sex might be almost as important as the quality of the skiing. The perfect resort would have at least one swinging disco, and preferably several. After all, there is such a thing as *après ski*.

So what is the perfect resort?

The best way to find the answer is to search for it. The quest is worth it. It is like finding the perfect

Both style and equipment have changed considerably since the 1920s, when the photograph on which this illustration is based was taken.

equipment for yourself. Either become your own expert on the matter or turn to experts on whose judgment experience has taught you that you can rely, experts who know your needs.

The quest, whether for equipment or resorts, is part of the fun of skiing. To view it otherwise is perhaps to be sadly disappointed. Even at that, no matter how well you are informed in advance of leaving for a fortnight's skiing vacation—what if the weather turns sour? At almost any place in ski country, rain can fall during a week's mild spell. The threat of avalanches can force the closure of the region's best skiing terrain. Wouldn't it be nice

ing for before you seek it. And other such homilies; they all apply.

Since resorts come in such profusion these years, with so many choices among superior choices, anyone starting out for the first time to take a skiing vacation is bound to be confused. The confusion dissipates when, as Plato said, thou knowest thyself. The better thou knowest thyself, and thy needs, the more assuredly will you find satisfaction and the right ski resort. Further on, this chapter raises most of the questions you should ask yourself, and your skiing vacation advisor.

Late-Victorian skiing on the streets of St. Moritz, already the winter-sports capital of Europe. Long dresses were mandatory until the 1920s, when the first daring ladies in breeches shocked the conventionally minded.

Ski Resorts
HOW THEY GREW

In the beginning, there were no ski resorts. There was only skiing as transportation. Around the middle of the last century, as leisure time became more available, the Scandinavians—principally the Norwegians—invented skiing as a sport, primarily one of jumping and touring. Then the Austrians devised means and equipment to adapt the game to their splendid Alps. But it remained for the Swiss to develop the winter resort, a place to go to ski. They were encouraged to do so by affluent British who yearned for sunshine in the winter. The Swiss merely winterized their previous creations, their Alpine summer retreats and tuberculosis *Kurhäuser*. At first, sledding and skating were the principal winter games. By the turn of the century, skiing had come along. Cog railways, funiculars, and aerial trams, which had been built for summer sightseers, became the first mechanized uphill conveyances for their winter visitors. The sport of alpine skiing was finally off and running.

Many well-established, world-famous European resorts still retain the original nineteenth-century flavor, partly in the Edwardian architecture of the old hotels, and unfortunately, partly in the bottlenecks of transportation created by streets and ski-lift networks that never envisioned the heavy traffic they would receive today. In Austria, Badgastein and Kitzbühel are prime examples. In Switzerland, there are Davos, St. Moritz, and Zermatt. In France, Chamonix might be added to this list.

By the 1920s, perhaps as many as fifty locales in Alpine Europe could call themselves ski resorts. Today, less than sixty years later, the European winter resorts have mushroomed into the hundreds. Around the world, at least 3,500–4,000 recognized places have been specifically improved, or developed from scratch, as skiers' playgrounds.

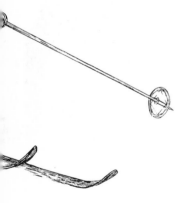

if your choice also featured indoor swimming pools, tennis courts, a large community of shops, casinos, and other distractions? Going too early or too late in the season can also lead to unhappiness. No people, no snow, no fun. But what is too early, too late?

And the slopes ... what if they are all too similar, or without sufficient challenge for the athletic experts in your entourage? Or too challenging for the less aggressive members?

Centuries ago, sages gave good advice for coping with such nettlesome questions: Forewarned is forearmed; be prepared; know what you are looking for before you seek it.

How can one generalize about so many places? Most have some individual characteristics, dictated by national heredity, of course, and by considerations of terrain, of snowfall, and of length of season. Any generalization about so much diversification will necessarily be sweeping, contain inaccuracies, and be unfair to some. Having said that, here is an examination of the various classes of ski centers, from the smallest to the largest.

To Switzerland goes credit for the development of the first winter ski resorts. These were entities that grew from previously established summer retreats that were health centers, built around the alleged curative powers of water from natural springs. This water was either hot, highly mineralized, radioactive, or all three.

Austria added a novel and important touch to the basic ski resort concept—the ski school. This was an idea brought to the fore by Hannes Schneider at the small village of St. Anton am Arlberg. We take ski school for granted now, knowing it to be an important part of any ski resort worthy of the name. But back in 1907, when Herr Schneider began to teach groups of people the art of controlling speed on skis, the idea was revolutionary. The logic for ski schools was simple: If you want skiers to bring you business, you'd better make people into skiers.

Today, of course, one can learn without the aid of ski school. But not nearly as fast as with its aid. A good instructor—and there are now tens of thousands around the world, all having passed rigorous national training and testing procedures—can make the difference between a good time on the slopes and, possibly, a disastrous time. Hence, the ski school is a necessary part of any ski resort, big or small.

Switzerland deserves yet another credit in the improvement of the ski resort. A man by the name of Constam invented a device resembling an upside-down T, or an old-fashioned ship's anchor, which was attached to an endless cable that went uphill and which literally pushed an upright skier along by the seat of the pants. The T-bar, being far less expensive than railways and aerial trams, was an instant success, and many T-bars are still in use. The newest ones are capable of moving uphill as many as 1,200 skiers per hour. The old ones, which are still found in older resorts, sometimes handle as few as 350 per hour, creating a source of real frustration for skiers enduring the often crowded conditions of today.

North America deserves the credit for developing an off-shoot of the skiing resort, and it is called

The world skiing atlas, with the ski spots marked by a star. A new star is added practically every year, and, nowadays, you can even ski in Hawaii and North Africa.

the ski area, being something less than a resort. What turned the trick was a Canadian device called the rope tow. Back in 1932, on a slope in the Laurentian Mountains about 30 miles (50 km) to the north of Montreal, an ardent skier backed up an old Ford car to the foot of a cleared, sloping pasture. He removed one of the rear-drive vehicle's rear tires, and with some ingenuity ran an endless rope from the drive wheel round an idle wheel up at the top of the slope. When the engine was fired up, the rope tow was born. It was an inexpensive way to get skiers up a slope. The art of climbing on skis now began its rapid decline. Yo-yo skiing was born: Ski up, ski down; ski up, ski down.

The rope tow provided an excellent means to strengthen the skiers' arms as they were pulled up slopes, some as long as 1,000 m (3,280 ft) and with

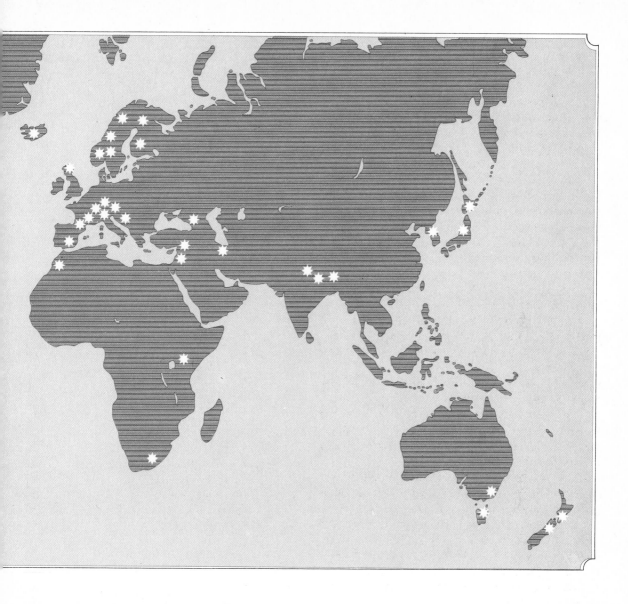

vertical drops in excess of 200 m (650 ft). Some ropes were arranged in series, so that really long runs were possible.

The idea of using the rope tow was imported into the United States, and by 1940, probably as many as four hundred ski areas using such devices were scattered around North America, principally in the more populated New England and Laurentian regions, and to the north and west of Chicago and Minneapolis.

Today, the ski area thrives all over the world, and, in particular, wherever skiable hills are close to urban population centers. Originally, the ski area had a rope tow and a base hut—a place to get warm, have a snack and a hot drink, and then again attack the slopes. Business was primarily on weekends; there were not enough skiers with lei-sure time to spare to keep the ski area populated on weekdays.

Then along came another invention—the created ski resort. Perhaps the first one anywhere went in at Sun Valley, Idaho, in 1936. Sestrière, Italy, was begun in 1934 but was not as complete a develop-ment as Sun Valley. The Union Pacific railroad wanted to build up its winter passenger-traffic business. Some kind of an attraction—a reason for people to travel—was needed. The company chose a superb place almost in the middle of nowhere, but not too far off its transcontinental rail lines. That place was Sun Valley, a delightful valley at 2,000 m (6,500 ft) base elevation, with rather rounded mountains swelling up to 3,000 m (10,000 ft). An entire village had to be created, since the nearby town of Ketchum was little more than a few buildings to service the needs of the local cowboys. Ranching was the region's prime reason for survival, though a small amount of gold mining had been carried on successfully in years past.

Sun Valley was to have it all: Formal and informal dining rooms, swimming pools of heated natural mineral water from nearby hot springs, a skating rink, bowling alleys, an opera house and a movie theater, a general store to cater to the needs of summer and winter guests, and accommodations for 800 guests, served by 800 staff members. The whole creation was immaculate, offering on the North American continent something akin to the graciousness of a Grand Palace hotel in Switzerland. It was to combine all this with the *gemütlich* flavor of an Austrian ski center of that time. The necessary ski school was staffed with the best of the times—Friedl Pfeifer, an Austrian world champion ski racer from St. Anton, and a dozen or two of his compatriots.

Sun Valley also brought to the skiing world another invention that was to radicalize our sport.

For uphill transportation, aerial trams were ruled out as being too costly, too susceptible to shutdowns due to high winds, and not safe enough for Americans. T-bars were not considered genteel enough, and rope tows were out of the question. Furthermore, both effectively truncate the terrain. At Sun Valley, as in most of the ski resorts of North America, trees cover the slopes all the way to the top. T-bars and rope tows would have required additional expensive and wasteful clearing of runs, or pistes, as they are known in Europe.

Sun Valley needed a unique solution. A Union Pacific engineer, who had designed overhead cable conveyor systems for the transport of bananas at the company's plantation in Guatemala, refined this design and came up with the world's first chair-lift. The contraption took people up the mountain by the seat of the pants, but not by dragging them on skis over the snow. Instead, they were seated and rode through the air. Thus, there was room for people to ski under the ski-lift riders, necessitating less clearing of the heavily wooded

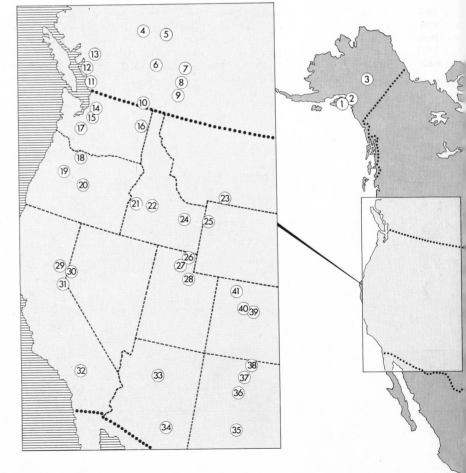

North American ski country. (*1*) Alyeska. (*2*) Arctic Valley. (*3*) Ski Land. (*4*) Cariboo Mountains. (*5*) Marmot Basin. (*6*) Monashee Mountains. (*7*) Lake Louise. (*8*) Bugaboo Mountains. (*9*) North Star Mountain. (*10*) Red Mountain. (*11*) Grouse Mountain. (*12*) Garibaldi/Whistler Mountain. (*13*) Mt. Seymour. (*14*) Stevens Pass. (*15*) Snoqualmie Summit. (*16*) Mt. Spokane. (*17*) White Pass Village. (*18*) Mt. Hood. (*19*) Hoodoo Ski Bowl. (*20*) Bachelor Butte/Mt. Bachelor. (*21*) Bogus Basin. (*22*) Sun Valley. (*23*) Red Lodge. (*24*) Kelly Canyon. (*25*) Jackson Hole. (*26*) Beaver Mountain. (*27*) Snow Basin. (*28*) Solitude/Brighton/Snowbird/Alta/Treasure Mountain. (*29*) Boreal Ridge/Squaw Valley/Heavenly Valley. (*30*) Incline Village/Slide Mountain. (*31*) Sugar Bowl. (*32*) Big Bear Lake. (*33*) Arizona Ski Bowl. (*34*) Mt. Lemmon. (*35*) Sierra Blanca. (*36*) Sandia Peak. (*37*) Santa Fe Basin.

conifer forests. And the cable and chairs could be kept at an elevation less than the height of the trees, meaning the wind would be less of an influencing factor. Riders could be swaddled in a blanket coat to counteract the sub-zero chill that hits the Rocky Mountains in January and February.

The Sun Valley idea of a created ski resort, totally planned for skiing in winter and vacationing in summer, was copied soon after at Mont Tremblant, Quebec, but on a smaller scale. By 1940, the chairlift had been copied at least a half-dozen times more, and the North American concept of a ski area grew a notch or two in the eyes of the skiing world.

Meanwhile, villages in the central European Alps seized on the success of skiing at the former summer-only resorts and began forming financial collectives to add aerial trams—and single chairlifts—to their villages, to haul skiers and sightseers from the bottoms of the deep valleys up to the sunnier shoulders of the mountains, from where the broad, open grazing and hay meadows, when

covered with snow, lent themselves beautifully to all kinds of skiing.

Then came World War II, with its obscene devastation of civilization (as if people that make war can be termed civilized!), and skiing as a sport did not really regain momentum until after 1950. By that time, a Frenchman by the name of Pomogalski had developed yet another type of uphill conveyance. This device required the skier to slip a disk the size of a bread-and-butter plate between the legs and allow himself to be hauled uphill. The Poma lift was cheaper than the T-bar, more flexible in that it could go round corners without too much additional expense, and required little manpower to operate.

The idea of the ski area spread and was imported wholesale into Europe, where ski areas were established right in or near existing resorts. Now, farmers could install lifts on their private lands and collect needed money in the wintertime. The price of alpine skiing became affordable for families. The old, established resort communities now began to

(*38*) Taos/Red River. (*39*) Evergreen/Eldora/Idlewild/Geneva Basin. (*40*) Aspen/Vail/Breckenridge/Snowmass/Copper Mountain.

(*41*) Steamboat Springs. (*42*) Mt. McKay/Mt. Baldy. (*43*) Big Powderhorn/Indian Head Mountains. (*44*) Searchmont Valley. (*45*) Laurentian Ski Club. (*46*) Mont Tremblant. (*47*) Mont St. Anne. (*48*) Cochand's.

(*49*) Bromont/Mont Sutton/Glen Mountain. (*50*) Sugarloaf Mountain. (*51*) Lost Valley/Pleasant Mountain. (*52*) Cannon Mountain/Mt. Cranmore/Loon Mountain/Mt. Whittier/Waterville/Mt. Tecumseh/Snow's Moun-

tain. (*53*) Gunstock. (*54*) Amherst/Brookline/Crotched Mountain/Fitzwilliam. (*55*) Mt. Sunapee/Bromley/Magic Mountain. (*56*) Killington/Pico Peak. (*57*) Stowe. (*58*) Lake Placid. (*59*) Gore Mountain. (*60*) Mt. Otsego/Scotch Valley. (*61*) Hunter Mountain/Mohawk Mountain. (*62*) Powder Hill. (*63*) Davos. (*64*) Camelback. (*65*) Mattaponi Slopes/Oregon Ridge. (*66*) The Homestead. (*67*) Gatlinburg. (*68*) Sheepback Mountain. (*69*) Deep Creek. (*70*) Seven Springs. (*71*) Blue Knob. (*72*) Boston Heights. (*73*) Snow Trails. (*74*) Valley High. (*75*) Twin Hearths/Chedoke. (*76*) Hidden Valley. (*77*) Mt. St. Louis/Horseshoe Valley. (*78*) Bay Motor Hotel Village/Beaver Valley/Talisman/Blue Mountain. (*79*) Boyne Highlands/Nub's Nob/Bellaire/Sugarloaf Mountain. (*80*) Alpine Valley. (*81*) Mt. Wawasee. (*82*) Little Switzerland. (*83*) Alpine Valley. (*84*) Chestnut Mountain. (*85*) Tyrol Basin.

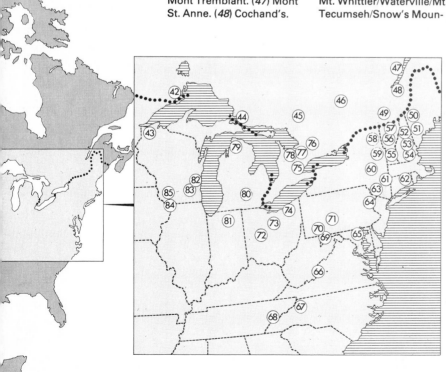

The famous mogul field at
Sun Valley, said by many
mogul fans to be the best
in the world.

144

Some of the many ski resorts in France. (*1*) Isola 2000/Auron. (*2*) Superbagnères. (*3*) La Mongie/Barèges. (*4*) Le Mont Dore. (*5*) Les Deux Alpes. (*6*) Alpe d'Huez. (*7*) Les Trois Vallées. (*8*) Valmorel. (*9*) La Plagne-Bellecôte. (*10*) La Clusaz. (*11*) Metabief. (*12*) Avoriaz. (*13*) Les Arcs/Flaine. (*14*) Argentière/Chamonix. (*15*) Val d'Isère-Tignes-Lac de Tignes. (*16*) St. Gervais. (*17*) Montgenèvre.

The number of Spanish ski resorts is increasing as the sport becomes more popular there. (*1*) La Molina/Nuria/Vallter 2.000. (*2*) Baqueira-Beret/Super-Espot/La Tuca. (*3*) Formigal/Panticosa/Candanchú. (*4*) Sierra de Gudar. (*5*) Solynieve. (*6*) Valdesqui/Navacerrada/La Pinilla/Valcotos. (*7*) Alto Campoo-Reinosa. (*8*) Pajares/San Isidro. (*9*) Cabeza de Manzaneda.

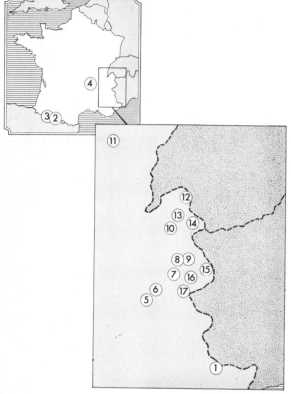

really become ski centers. Kitzbühel, Austria, was one of the first resorts to develop what the Austrians call a *Zircus*—a circuit where one could cover a wide area of skiable terrain via a series of interconnected ski lifts of all types—aerial trams, chairlifts, and some sort of a drag-lift. By 1960, skiing was no longer something to be considered as a way of life for escapists trying to flee from the rigors of urban living. The sport had become an economically feasible enterprise.

Internationally famous ski spas were now well entrenched and successful. Austria had its Badgastein, St. Anton, Zürs, Lech, and Kitzbühel. New developments were emerging around Innsbruck, Zell am See, and in fact, in almost all of the great Alpine valleys that run down to the Inn River—the Paznauntal, the Comperdell, the Ötztal, etc.

Switzerland's old gems were blossoming, too: St. Moritz, Davos, Zermatt, of course; but also Grindelwald, Wengen, Mürren, Arosa, Gstaad, Klosters, Crans-Montana, Andermatt, Flims, to mention only the top spots; and new places like Verbier and Anzers were beginning to be spoken of. Also, the scenic countryside was gradually becoming dotted with cosy family resorts that were more or less European-style ski areas.

Germany, of course, had its Garmisch-Partenkirchen, and several other burgeoning locales, such as Oberstdorf, on the north flank of the pre-Alps.

France was well entrenched with Chamonix Valley, tucked in deeply at the base of Europe's highest peak, the 4,810-m (15,780 ft) Mont Blanc, as well as with Val d'Isère and the gathering-spot of the cinema *chic*, Megève. New developments were coming to the fore, also: Courchevel, Avoriaz, Tignes, to name the more important.

Italy had Cortina, Sestrière, Courmayeur, Breuil-Cervinia on its side of the Matterhorn, and several hundred other places big and small. With its generally milder climate, easier skiing, and rapidly improving ski developments, this country took its place as a destination for the true skier.

North America had its Aspen, its Sun Valley, its Mont Tremblant, and its Stowe, but not too many other good places that could be designated as skiing resorts, although almost five hundred ski areas were now extant.

The 1960s were crystallizing and consolidating years for the development of skiing. Resorts and ski areas made capital improvements, enlarging parking lots and replacing old, single-passenger chair-lifts with ones with double seats. But in the main, they sat back and enjoyed the fruits of their labors. Except in France.

France made the big breakthrough in those years, planting seeds which, in the 1970s, would bear fruit that would now, in the 1980s, begin to reach maturity.

The following are among the most famous of the Swiss Alps resorts. (*1*) Klosters. (*2*) Davos. (*3*) Arosa. (*4*) St. Moritz. (*5*) Pontresina. (*6*) Silvaplana. (*7*) Flims/Laax. (*8*) Andermatt. (*9*) Engelberg. (*10*) Grindelwald. (*11*) Wengen. (*12*) Mürren/Jungfraujoch. (*13*) Saas Fee. (*14*) Zermatt. (*15*) Verbier. (*16*) Lenk/Adelboden. (*17*) Crans-Montana. (*18*) Gstaad/Les Diablerets. (*19*) Villars. (*20*) Champéry.

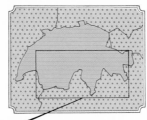

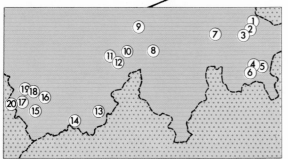

people to the mountains—the solitude, the scenery, the open spaces. It would be far more beneficial to consolidate those spread-out, single-family dwelling units into one or several large units that rose high into the sky. By so doing, only one road would need to be built. Problems of snow removal could be vastly diminished, since parking would be provided underneath the main edifice. Great savings in the use of heat could be effected by keeping shops of all types indoors, in pedestrian malls which would interconnect with the lodgings, restaurants, and uphill conveyance terminals. By so doing, the mountain environment, the lands surrounding the ski places, would be left virtually untouched. Only towers to support the uphill conveyances would interrupt the terrain.

And so the idea of the created, modern super-resort was born, replete with its condominiums and efficiency apartments.

But where to build this new type of super-resort, which is a sort of city within itself? Obviously, not down in the old villages, where the sun shines for only brief hours during the short winter days, where traffic was already snarled, and where open

The French government was concerned about the declining populations of smaller communities in the mountains and also felt that France should enjoy a larger share of the ever-increasing numbers of tourists and skiers to the Alpine countries. French leaders were concerned, too, about the almost impossible congestion and pollution occurring in the old villages due to the tremendous hordes of automobiles brought there not just in the summer, but in the winter. These problems were by no means unknown in Austria, Switzerland, and Italy. So an agency was created in France to study the development of tourism in the Alps, principally those of Savoie and Haute Savoie, but not to the exclusion of the Maritime Alps and the Pyrenees. One result of the agency's work was that long-term, low-interest loans were made available to entrepreneurial businessmen for new developments in these areas. But this new agency also went further. It studied problems of pollution, congestion, and, in some places, the proliferation of single-family dwellings and chalets. It concluded that such types of development created their own worst headaches. Roads had to interconnect single-family units, and what could be more disruptive to the local environment than roads and air-polluting vehicles?

Further, the agency decided that it was pointless to destroy those qualities which originally attracted

Alpine skiing in Germany is concentrated to the southern part of the country and to the mountain areas in the Black Forest. (*1*) Forbach. (*2*) Baiersbronn. (*3*) Lenzkirch/Saig/Kappel/Feldberg/Muggenbunn. (*4*) Wiesental. (*5*) Herrischried. (*6*) Immenstadt/Rettenberg/Kranzegg. (*7*) Fischen/Bolsterlang/Ofterschwang/Balderschwang. (*8*) Schwangau/Pfronten/Nesselwang. (*9*) Garmisch-Partenkirchen. (*10*) Mittenwald. (*11*) Lenggries. (*12*) Tegernsee Tal. (*13*) Kufstein/Oberaudorf/Kiefers- welden/Hochek/Kaisertal. (*14*) Chiemgau/Aschau/Sachrang. (*15*) Ruhpolding. (*16*) Berchtesgaden.

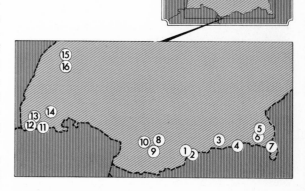

lands for parking and building were as scarce as snow in hell. The place to build was up high on the shoulders of the mountains themselves, up where the good snow fields really began, up where the scenery was truly magnificent. The French call the resulting residential–commercial edifices *paquebots des neiges*—steamships of the snows, a most apt phrase.

The first of these new, or third-generation, resorts was at Courchevel. Its only failures, according to French experts on such matters, were that the government omitted to secure all the developable and skiable lands in the vicinity, and then permitted the development of private chalets and roads. The overall control and management of the resort was thus lost, and private developments sprouted quickly, often in inappropriate locations. However, Courchevel has been an immense success, along with its interconnected satellites, Méribel-les-Allues, Les Ménuires, and Val Thorens.

This vast region of totally master-planned ski developments is collectively known as *Les Trois Vallées* ("the three valleys"). However, there are, in fact, at least five valleys—more if you count the lesser condominium and apartment settlements. There are at least 125 assorted ski-lifts and in excess of 290 km (180 miles) of marked trails and slopes in the complex. There is probably no better interconnection of lifts and ski trails to be found

A skiing holiday will give you many experiences, but none so fine as that of skiing down wooded slopes. Remember that the ski resort must be below the tree-line.

anywhere. Now, *that* is a ski circuit to end all "ski *Zircusse*"!

But is it? France has at least one other region that comes close, and that may soon catch up with or even surpass Les Trois Vallées. That is the complex at Val d'Isère–Tignes–Lac de Tignes. This region of high-country skiing does not offer the same back and forth skiability as does Les Trois Vallées, since you go from east to west quite easily, but not quite as easily on the return trip. Here, such long-distance journeying is not for new skiers, since the snow usually is not groomed and some of the pitches are unusually steep. Experience and ability are prerequisites for taking full advantage of Val's opportunities.

France has other totally created ski areas. Among these are Les Arcs and La Plagne-Bellecôte, both ski centers with over thirty ski lifts apiece and amenities to match. About a hundred ski resorts dot the map of France, most of them located from the Jura Mountains north of Geneva (which is in that part of Switzerland that sticks into France) and down the spine of the Alps to within 80 km (50 miles) of Nice.

Excellent skiing and good ski resorts are also to be found in the Pyrenees on both sides of the French-Spanish border. Actually, this region is often referred to by ski historians as the birthplace of French skiing, the terrain having been explored on skis as early as 1901. Lack of transport by rail and road has delayed development in this region. However, there are already fourteen developed ski areas on the French side. On the Spanish side, there are many small resorts that cater mainly for Spanish skiers, but Baqueira-Beret is one that will soon join the ranks of the internationally great resorts. Spain's largest international ski area is, of course, Solynieve, in the Sierra Nevada, a couple of hours' drive from Granada or Malaga. At 3,400 m (11,800 ft), Solynieve has a long skiing season and is much appreciated for its sunshine.

In the 1970s, Switzerland took a cue from France and began to upgrade the quality of its old resorts, while at the same time doing its utmost to retain its heritage of centuries-old farming villages. No completely new resorts have been created, but several old villages have been totally refurbished and thoroughly modernized in terms of skiing facilities.

One such is Verbier, in the southwest Valais

Italy's ski resorts are dotted all round its northern borders. (*1*) Limone-Piemonte/Colle di Tenda. (*2*) Sauze-d'Oulx. (*3*) Sestrière/Bardonecchia. (*4*) Courmayeur. (*5*) Breuil-Cervinia. (*6*) Alagna-Valsésia. (*7*) Macugnaga. (*8*) Madesimo. (*9*) Sondrio. (*10*) Livigno. (*11*) Bormio. (*12*) Prad-StilfserJoch. (*13*) Alleghe-Malga Ciapela. (*14*) Val Gardena. (*15*) Ponte di Legno/Passo di Tonale. (*16*) Madonna di Campiglio. (*17*) Marmolada. (*18*) Cortina. (*19*) Monte Bondone.

region of the country. Verbier exemplifies another characteristic of the modern resort, carried to near perfection by the French, but not exclusive to them. Many resorts and ski villages in Switzerland have vastly expanded their skiing terrain by adding interconnecting ski lifts. Verbier, for example, is ski-connected to the neighboring towns of Haute Nendaz and Thyon. Gstaad has several such connections, and if a kilometer or two by road is included, it makes the high glacier regions of Les Diablerets part of the Gstaad complex. Similarly, Flims joins with Laax, Crans with Montana, and Lenk with Adelboden. And the list goes on. One can ski from Zermatt into Breuil-Cervinia in Italy; from Champéry, also in Switzerland, into the French resort of Avoriaz. It is almost impossible to describe adequately the grandeur of Swiss skiing resorts, most of which have incredibly fine possibilities for cross-country jaunts, day-long excursions, and even some of the world's best overnight, high-country ski mountaineering.

Ever since Hannes Schneider won world acclaim for his ability to teach skiers that speed is the thrill, but control is the art, Austrian resorts have had a

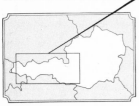

Some of Austria's many resorts. (*1*) Sachsenburg. (*2*) Oberdrauburg. (*3*) Mallnitz. (*4*) Badgastein. (*5*) Wagrain. (*6*) Obertauern. (*7*) Schladming. (*8*) Hinterstoder. (*9*) Ramsau. (*10*) Lofer. (*11*) Maria Alm. (*12*) Zell am See/Kaprun/Bruck.

(*13*) Uttendorf. (*14*) Saalbach/Hinterglemm. (*15*) St. Johann. (*16*) Kitzbühel. (*17*) Jochberg. (*18*) Söll. (*19*) Alpbach. (*20*) Neukirchen. (*21*) Mayrhofen. (*22*) Innsbruck (Igls, Mutters, Axams-Lizum). (*23*) Seefeld. (*24*) Hintertux/Steineck. (*25*) Neustift. (*26*) Sölden/Hochgurgl/Obergurgl/Ötztal. (*27*) Serfaus. (*28*) Nauders. (*29*) Ischgl. (*30*) St. Anton. (*31*) Gaschurn. (*32*) Zürs/Lech.

major place in the scheme of things. St. Anton is justifiably world famous, and new ski lifts on previously undeveloped mountains keep enhancing its appeal. Kitzbühel still has excellent interconnect skiing, as do the villages of Zürs and Lech.

During the 1950s and 1960s, the further development of Austrian skiing lagged way behind that of France, Switzerland, and even of Italy. However, during the 1970s, Austrian resort developments began to advance steadily. Several new and exciting ski terrains have been mechanized, principally in the southwest corner of the Tyrol province. Among the Austrian additions to the ranks of world class resorts, Obergurgl at the south end of the Ötztal must be mentioned.

At least another dozen Austrian regions are worthy of mention and could be included on any serious skier's must-ski-someday list. What they lack in grandeur and scope, they make up for in quaintness, charm, and the ability to please all but the most fastidious and expert of skiers. In terms of moving forward the development of the ski resort, there is little to be said for Austria, which has contented itself with regularly leading when it comes to superior ski racers, ski techniques, and ski equipment, not to its ski resort development.

Italy, another country of world-class ski resorts, also has not advanced (until the last few years) the state of the art of ski resorts, although in the mid-1930s, Italy was probably the first to strive for the newly created, purpose-designed ski resort. Such resorts were erected at Sestrière, near the borders of the Maritime Alps of France, and at Cortina, in the Dolomites. Sestrière in recent years has become one of the greatest interconnected ski complexes, with its link-up to the French border resort of Montgenèvre. This *Via Latea*, as it is called, is a very close second to Les Trois Vallées. Another world-class complex can be found in the South Tyrol at Val Gardena, where a half-dozen ski villages have linked up to form the *Sella Ronda*, a loop of downhill skiing and ski lifts in excess of 50 km (30 miles). The Italians must be credited for simplifying the use of ski-lift tickets. For a fixed fee, a skier may buy a plastic card that is good for as many as 150 ski lifts within a region; all the skier has to do is to slip it into an electronic device before each uphill departure. The device automatically prorates and tabulates the use, so that the various owning companies of the many ski lifts may, at the end of the season, equitably divide the gross receipts.

Italy should not be erased from anyone's future ski itinerary. At least two dozen of the resorts there are worthy of international status. Among these are Bormio, Sauze-d'Oulx, Madesimo, and Madonna di Campiglio.

Meanwhile, in the United States, business methods began to be applied to the management of ski developments. In the 1970s, the uncertainties of snowfall, the vagaries of weather, the negative effects of wind on newly fallen snow (that is, by blowing it off the runs and into the trees), and the effect of other unpredictables upon the economic status of a ski resort provoked new developments of considerable importance. One was the creation of snow-making machines—a series of "snow-guns" which blow out at high velocity a mixture of pressurized air and water, which, upon meeting with temperatures a degree or two below freezing and with low relative humidities, immediately turns to snow. Many formerly marginally skiable grounds were now capable of providing good skiing. The lower slopes at many of the big resorts, which often offered scratchy and rocky skiing during early and late season, could now be adequately covered with snow. Additionally, the development

Ski resorts in Scandinavia. (*1*) Kongsberg. (*2*) Rjukan. (*3*) Norefjell. (*4*) Gol/Hemsedal. (*5*) Geilo. (*6*) Voss. (*7*) Galdhöpiggen. (*8*) Stryn. (*9*) Sunne/Torsby/Hovfjället. (*10*) Sälen. (*11*) Idre (*12*) Tänndalen (*13*) Funäsdalen/Vemdalen/Lofsdalen. (*14*) Åre/Duved/ Storlien. (*15*) Tärnaby. (*16*) Dundret. (*17*) Riksgränsen. (*18*) Rovaniemi. (*19*) Suomutunturi. (*20*) Viitasaari. (*21*) Kuopio/Nilsiä. (*22*) Vammala. (*23*) Lahti.

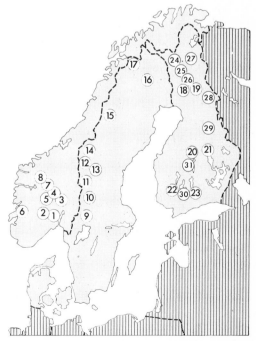

of a purpose vehicle—snowcats in America, ratracs in much of Europe—made it possible to pack into place all those flakes which might otherwise disappear into the woods at the first signs of a breeze. Further, these snowcats were equipped with a wide variety of devices to claw up icy surfaces, pulverize lumpy, crusty snow, and eradicate what to some skiers are pesky intrusions on a ski slope—moguls.

As a result of such improvements, the lowly ski area, as well as the big resort—sometimes open, sometimes closed, all because, like farmers, they were totally dependent upon the weather—have become capitally expensive developments. One large snowcat with auxiliary equipment costs almost U.S. $60,000 (£30,000). A snow-making system to cover an area of 100 acres (4 hectares) costs about U.S. $2 million (£1 million), including all the necessary air compressors, water pumps, cooling towers, and miles-long network of plumbing and hoses to service the snowguns.

In Scandinavia, the winter is long, lasting from October almost to May in the more northern parts, and Norway, Sweden, and Finland have given

The best of today's ski resorts have facilities for all
levels of skiing skill. This
panoramic view of a resort
shows the various slopes,
graded according to their
difficulty: black for very
difficult slopes, red for difficult, and blue for easy.
The lifts indicated are:
J- or T-bar or Poma lift:
gondola car:
cable car:

much to alpine skiing, although they have not been
to the forefront in the development of ski resorts.

Norway has thousands of kilometers of prepared
cross-country ski trails, a decent percentage of
which is lit for night skiing. But it also has at least
one ski station of international repute, and that is
Voss, which lies less than two hours by train from
the west-coast city of Bergen. Voss has hosted
World Cup competitions several times in the past
decade and has become popular with German,
British, and Danish skiers. Also popular among
these skiers is Geilo, between Oslo and Bergen. At

Japan's well-frequented resorts. (1) Furano. (2) Sapporo/Teine Olympia. (3) Niseko Plateau Hirafu. (4) Zao/Tengendai Azuma. (5) Inawashiro. (6) Kusatsu Onsen/Shiga Heights. (7) Happo-one.

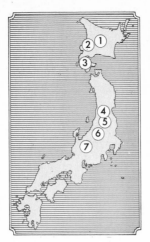

Geilo, the ski lifts take skiers to an altitude of 1,200 m (3,930 ft). Some additional three dozen ski areas are scattered throughout the region between Bergen and Oslo. The friendliness of the Norwegian people to most strangers make up for the lack of any great ski-resort developments, although the 1980s will see major strides taken in this area.

Sweden has imported the American concept of the ski area, and villages all over the middle and north of the country are installing ski lifts. The best-known resort is at Åre/Duved, where a not-always-easy descent of 1,000 m (3,280 ft) is available. Summer skiing is to be had at Riksgränsen, in the far north of the country.

In Finland, as in Norway and Sweden, most skiers (that is, most people) ski where there is snow. The terrain of all three countries is ideal for crosscountry skiing, and the skiing tradition is so strong there that, should snow not fall some winter, everyone would still put on skis and head for the nearest patch of frosted grass. Finland has a handful of alpine ski resorts, the most memorable resort being Suomutunturi, where the Arctic Circle cuts through the dining area of the hotel's main lodge. Soumutunturi has a ski lift that serves a vertical of 300 m (980 ft).

Poland has a half-dozen developments scattered all over the north flank of the Tatra Mountains. The most famous resort is Zakopane, a year-round tourist center. While delightful to many, and comparatively easy on the wallet, the Polish resorts and the half-dozen over the border on the Czechoslovakian side would best be left to either the skier-traveler or those not spoiled by the high degree of mechanization and sophistication offered by the resorts of Western Europe and North America.

The same may be said of the few developments in the Carpathian and Transylvanian mountains of Rumania, the Urals and Altais of Russia, the Caucasus in Iran, Turkey, and Russia, and resorts in similarly exotic parts of the world. And that includes Scotland, where three or four highland ski centers are located in the Grampian mountains between Inverness and Dundee.

There are also ski resorts and day areas in Yugoslavia, Bulgaria, and Greece, though none of these countries can be said to have added anything to the advancement of the ski resort. But they are reflections of just how popular a sport skiing has become.

All in all, the ski area has come of age.

And so has the ski resort. Today, there are more scattered around the world than any one person could possibly visit adequately in a lifetime. May your quest for the perfect resort be as fulfilling as it has been for many of your fellow skiers, whether you settle on, say, a neighborhood ski area, a quiet retreat deep in some secluded Alpine valley, a boisterous, internationally famous super-complex, or the ultimate in skiing—by helicopter. To each his own.

(LEFT) The New Zealand ski resorts. (1) Mt. Ruapehu. (2) Mt. Egmont. (3) Mt. Cook.

(BELOW) Skiing in Australia is confined to the southeast corner and to Tasmania. (1) Thredbo/Mt. Perisher/Smiggin Holes/Charlotte Pass. (2) Mt. Buller. (3) Falls Creek/Mt. Bogong.

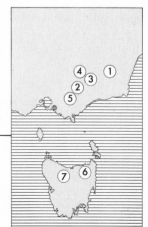

(4) Mt. Buffalo/Mt. Hotham. (5) Mt. Baw-Baw. (6) Ben Lomond. (7) Cradle Mountain.

To Each His Own

SELECTING YOUR SKI RESORT

Where in the world should I ski? Austria or Australia, Spain or Sicily, Czechoslovakia or Yugoslavia, Canada or Japan, Italy or France?

Actually, in your own backyard, either literally or figuratively, is a good place to start. The fact is that, wherever there are hills and snow, alpine skiing is possible. A very fat book indeed would be needed to chronicle adequately all of the world's ski resorts.

At first, the choice is staggering. But as you consider your or your family's needs, the options begin to narrow down. Practical considerations, based on objective criteria, must be dealt with. Such things as your budget, accessibility of your intended destination, mode of travel to it, languages spoken, amount of time available to you, and characteristics of the resort itself must be taken into account. Obviously, such a treatise as this can only deal in generalities, but knowing them will help you to interpret properly the lavish travel brochures and to ask your travel agent the right questions.

Know Thyself

A fascinating aspect of skiing is that as your skills improve so does your measure for pleasure. Yet at the same time, the game is fun from the start, provided that you have good equipment and that you take ski lessons. Rent or hire your ski gear initially, say, for the first week of your skiing career. After that, you will have a good idea of just how precisely your ski boots must fit, what type of skis and bindings you would like, and so on. You may start your career at one of the internationally famous ski resorts, or you may do it at one of the smallest of ski areas. My advice is to opt for the latter, since the big resorts can so flood you with their grandeur, and with the skiing expertise of their clientele, that you may be continually frustrated by your assumed inadequacies. Even the smallest of resorts—with a vertical drop of as little as 300 m (1,000 ft)—usually have enough variety to keep any first-timer happy for the first week.

At the end of a week of lessons, consider yourself an intermediate. You are possibly entering a period of great frustration. You may possess the basic technical skills, sufficient to make decent skidded turns when conditions of snow are near ideal and when the run is not too steep. But once you get off the incubator slopes generally used for first timers, you will find that the snow is often less than ideal and that the big slopes up above sometimes are frighteningly steep. You will lack the experience to cope with such situations and, possibly, you will also lack the necessary strength in the right muscles. For that reason, the biggest of resorts might well be shunned, unless they are frequently groomed by snowcats. In general, you would be happiest skiing at locations where the vertical potential is no greater than 500 m (1,640 ft).

Consider yourself an advanced skier after you have had about a hundred hours of actual down-mountain time. That would be in your third or fourth season, under normal circumstances, considering that for every hour you are on a mountain, less than half of it is spent actually skiing. As an advanced skier, you will want to visit a ski resort where the slopes offer some challenge to your ability, with a lot of variety and a vertical potential approaching 1,000 m (3,280 ft). Any of the internationally famous places will have slopes which do that, as will a vast number of less famous resorts.

It usually takes at least five years to become an expert skier, and maybe ten, unless you have been fortunate enough to ski, actually move downhill, at least a hundred hours per season. Of course, if you are an expert, you will have a good idea of where to go for steep, challenging terrain and where the powder snow lies deepest. Word of mouth from fellow skiers will have whetted your appetite. Not all of the world-class resorts offer such challenges.

On the elaborate maps put out by ski resorts and showing the locations of ski lifts and runs, black lines are usually used to designate terrain to challenge the experts, red lines to indicate more moderate terrain suitable for advanced and better intermediates, and blue lines to indicate the easiest way down.

Your Personal Needs

What languages do you speak? Some parts of the world are notoriously poor in translating abilities. In North America, most people speak English only. Some French and German is spoken at ski resorts, particularly at Vail, Aspen, and Stowe. But, in non-English-speaking countries, don't count on being able to communicate with too many of the key personnel or with the many people you will have to rely on for moving from plane to car to hotel, etc. In France, German is not too popular a language, and in Austria, French is seldom spoken, but English is understood at most resorts. If you are not an experienced traveler or do not like the idea of having to communicate in languages other than those with which you are familiar, then you had best seek ski resorts where you have been assured language will not be a barrier.

What will your budget be? A ski resort is first of all a resort. Automatically, that implies higher prices. The most famous places will be the most expensive, although with perseverance, less expensive ways of staying at them can be found. In the old, well-established resorts, hotels are every bit as posh and fastidious as they are in big cities. They are likely to be more expensive. Austria has many *Pensions*—private rooms in private homes, a situation which might very well suit families that enjoy togetherness at not too great a cost. Many hotels will expect you to take all your meals there, or at least two of them. Not necessarily so in North America. Most European resorts have hotels that offer breakfast only, although they often have restaurant facilities.

At many of the newer ski stations, hotels are disappearing from the scene; in their place are condominiums and self-service efficiency apartments where you may do your own cooking. They are usually very compact and provide the maximum amount of sleeping facilities in the minimum amount of space.

How close to the ski lifts do you wish to be? The greatest convenience is to be very close to the ski slopes, but expect to pay more for it. Prices for lodging tend to vary with the distance away from the uphill conveyances—the further away, the cheaper. Parents especially appreciate the convenience of being able to dress their children, supply them with their tickets, and turn them loose to the immediate out-of-doors—to their ski instructor.

Will you be bringing your family along? If the youngest of your clan cannot attend ski school, be sure a nursery is available. Should your children be less than in their middle teen years, it is best not to attend one of the big super complexes or even one of the larger spas. Many "family" style resorts are to be found. These are large enough to satisfy the skiing needs of the parents, yet not so big that parents cannot swoop down to the lesser slopes to check on the progress of the youngsters. Generally, smallness is friendlier than bigness.

How will you travel to your destination? At most of the more popular destinations, traffic congestion is horrendous, especially on weekends and if the resort is within an hour or two of a metropolitan region. At some, you may need a private vehicle to get from village to ski lifts. At others, Zermatt for example, no vehicles are permitted into the resort. When making your plans, best inquire very

(*ABOVE*) Summer skiing can be found in many areas that have high elevations. This picture shows an exotic form of summer skiing—midsummer skiing in the midnight sun at Riksgränsen, Sweden.

(*BELOW*) Once you have felt the thrill of skiing deep powder, you will want your skiing holidays to be in places where there are good chances of deep powder.

carefully about the availability of transportation. Why take a car if it will only be in the way once there, and if rail transportation takes you directly there? Forget about train travel in North America, except for big-city commuter service. Since transportation to and from your destination may well account for half of your total vacation expenses, it is wise to research the alternatives thoroughly.

When will you take your vacation? Almost all of the world's favorite places are booked solid at Christmas-time and for at least a year in advance. Similarly at Easter, especially if it falls in March. High season, which is usually in February and March, may also be a very difficult time to book space.

Generally, snow comes to the highest mountains the earliest of all and stays the latest. Resorts in the European Alps that offer skiing at or near 3,000 m (10,000 ft) may well have skiing—good skiing—in late November, but rarely sooner. October skiing is a rarity almost anywhere in the world. Those resorts with base elevations less than 2,000 m

(6,500 ft) may have pretty scratchy skiing—if any—even at Christmas. Snow-making machines could alter that situation for the better. January is usually the coldest month, and in many places, the stormiest. Many resorts at lower elevations may cease operations by March, unless the ski lifts reach up into colder terrain. The higher stations offer the most pleasant weather in March and April. The highest places will have skiing through May, and even all summer, especially if a skiable glacier is near at hand.

Summer skiing? Indeed, it is possible in at least two dozen regions of the high Alps, from Austria through Italy and Switzerland to France, in Norway, Sweden, and in a few places in western North America. Also, you may recall that on the other side of the Equator the seasons are reversed. June is akin to December, September to March. There is excellent skiing, of limited elite-class standards, at Portillo, Chile. Less exciting but still excellent resorts are to be found in San Carlos de Bariloche, Argentina. Both New Zealand and Australia have

good skiing, and the sport is becoming very popular there. In Australia, there are several good resorts in the Mount Kosciusco State Park, among them Thredbo, Mount Perisher, and Charlotte Pass, while another good area for skiing is near Bright, in Victoria, where skiing at about 1,500 m (5,000 ft) is to be had, especially at Mount Buffalo and Mount Hotham. In New Zealand, there are great opportunities for high-country ski mountaineering in the Mount Cook area, where skiing groups are flown in to any one of the twenty-seven peaks that are above 3,000 m (10,000 ft). The ski resort of Chateau Tongariro, in the Mount Ruapehu region, offers very good slopes between about 1,300 m (4,500 ft) and 2,200 m (7,200 ft). Other well-known resorts are Coronet Peak and Mount Egmont.

How much social life will you require? Smaller ski areas and resorts do not have a very active night life. But not everyone needs one. Learning skiers may be so tired by dinner-time that rest may be even more important than food. Others may pace themselves on the *piste*, all the better to savor the delights of *cherchez la femme, ou l'homme*. Discos abound in the poshest of places. Most resorts worthy of the name feature at least one. The largest winter spas may also have curling rinks, skating rinks, riding stables, casinos, public swimming-pools, and of course, inviting shops, where it is all too easy to lighten the weight of your wallet.

Is the travel experience of equal or greater importance to you than the skiing? Skiing is to be had in many exotic places of the world: Turkey, Iran, the Lebanon, and other countries of the Middle East. India even has two ski resorts. But these are of very minor consequence in terms of skiing experience. You may travel to Chalcaltya, in Bolivia, if you want to ski above 5,000 m (16,400 ft), but bring lots of aspirin—or your own oxygen supply! And, of course, Japan has hundreds of mechanized ski areas, the most famous of them being Sapporo, Zao, and Chikakogen; for the American or British skier, it is the travel experience that would be exciting and exotic, of course. Scandinavians are friendly, and skiing in their countries is socially very rewarding. North America is extremely large, and the West is filled with natural wonders—the Grand Canyon, the desert mountains of Monument Valley, the ancient cliff dwellings of lost civilizations. All of these are within a day's drive of the great ski resorts in Utah—Snowbird, Park City—and of Jackson Hole in Wyoming. Big-mountain skiing at Whistler Mountain is only two hours away from the beautiful port city of Vancouver, British Columbia. Ski, and travel—it's a magnificent way to see the world.

Resort Selection: Zeroing In

1 Beg, buy, borrow, or steal a good guide to the ski resorts in the region you wish to ski.

2 Visit, or write to, the government tourist offices of those countries you would like to visit and request their literature on ski resorts. Some air carriers also have excellent guides for free distribution.

3 Visit a travel agency and request further information about the resorts that specifically interest you, or write directly to the resort associations of your choice and request their brochures.

4 Study the brochures carefully. Be aware that at some of the resorts all the ski lifts indicated may not be in operation. Some of the smaller stations are prone to include proposed lifts in their publicity material. Some fail to indicate that certain lifts are no longer in operation, or that they only operate in late season, when the snows are deep enough. All too often, those seemingly nice interconnections are not in existence—they only seem that way because the artist who drew up the mountain plan had to use artistic license in interpreting the terrain.

5 Request your agent to provide full details of where you will be staying. Will you be close to the ski lifts? Is there scheduled transportation from your hotel to the slopes and back? Will you be in the main building, or in a more distant annex? Will you have a bathtub or a shower, or no attached bathroom? Verify all details of transportation.

6 Carefully assess what extra costs you will incur. Allow at least ten percent more than your estimates, take a second mortgage on your home, a deep breath, and leave for one of life's great pleasures—skiing.

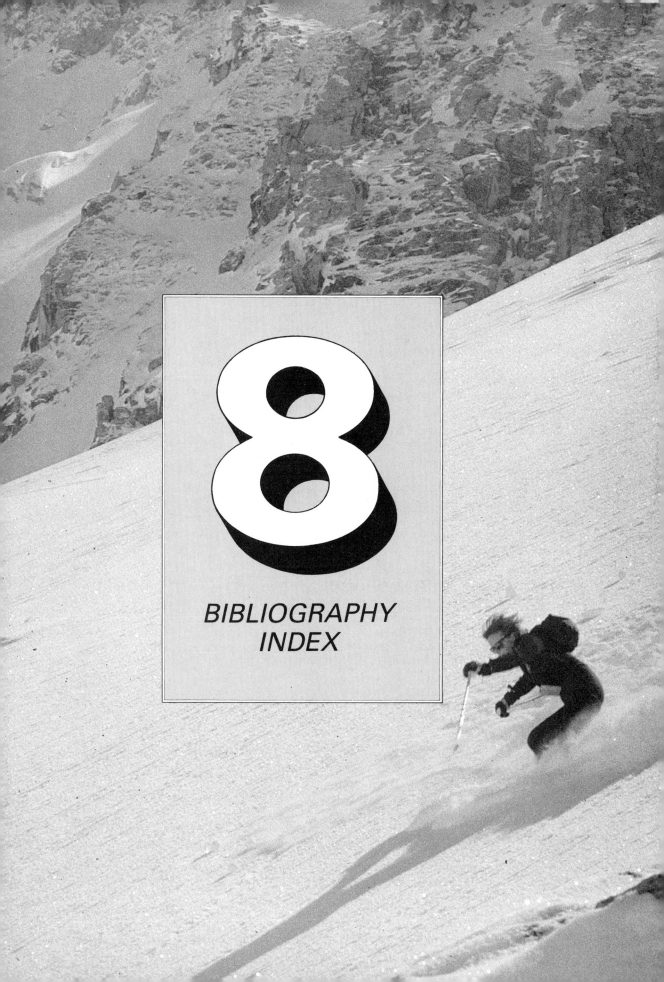

8
BIBLIOGRAPHY
INDEX

BIBLIOGRAPHY

Abraham, Horst. *American Teaching Method.* Vail, 1974.

Campbell, Stu. *Ski with the Big Boys.* New York, 1974.

Eriksson, Anders; Forsberg, Artur; Källberg, Lars; Tesch, Per; and Karlsson, Jan. *Alpint.* Idrottsfysiologi, rapport nr 17. Stockholm, 1977.

Flower, Raymond. *The Story of Ski-ing and Other Winter Sports.* London, 1976.

Garzanti e il Coni per lo sport. *Il Libro dello Sci.* Milan, 1974.

Joubert, Georges. *Teach Yourself to Ski.* Translated by Sim Thomas. Aspen, 1970.

Joubert, Georges. *Le Ski, un art, un technique.* Paris, 1979.

Joubert, Georges, and Vuarnet, Jean. *How to Ski the New French Way.* Translated by Sim Thomas and John Fry. New York, 1969.

Kemmler, Jürgen, and Vorderwülbecke, Manfred. *The Complete Skiing Handbook.* Translated by Martin Dunitz Limited. London, 1979.

Mohan, John; Hiltner, Walt; and Barthel, Bruce. *Freestyle Skiing.* New York, 1976.

Oddo, Guido. *La Tecnica dello Sci.* Novara, 1977.

Sanders, R. J. *The Anatomy of Skiing and Powder Skiing.* Denver, 1976.

Schultes, Hermann. *Principles of Modern Ski Design.* Middletown, 1978.

The Sunday Times. *We Learned to Ski.* London, 1974.

Witherell, Warren. *How the Racers Ski.* New York, 1972.

INDEX